Life Changes while Grieving

Three Significant Changes. One Ultimate Outcome.

Author of *In a Heartbeat*

DOMINIC MURGIDO

ISBN 979-8-89043-482-1 (paperback)
ISBN 979-8-89043-483-8 (digital)

Christian Faith Publishing
832 Park Avenue
Meadville, PA 16335
www.christianfaithpublishing.com

Printed in the United States of America

To those who have lost a loved one and continue
to live with the heartache and sorrow that grief
produces, may you find peace, grace, and comfort
while keeping your loved one close to your heart.

Also by Dominic Murgido

*In a Heartbeat: A Tale of Reflection, Faith,
Hope, and Resilience* (a memoir)

Miss Your Forever: Reflections after the Death of a Spouse

Praise for In a Heartbeat

In a Heartbeat exemplifies the meaning of post-traumatic growth. Through his honesty and vulnerability, the author takes us on his grief journey beginning with the traumatic death of his wife, Sue. He is able to convey all of the feelings associated with challenges he faced along the way as well as with each of his steps forward. His story of finding meaning in his life after everything had changed is truly inspirational. I highly recommend it to those who are grieving or to those who wish to better understand grief.

—Pam W., certified grief educator

In a Heartbeat speaks of the details behind the grief story with the raw emotion that was being experienced and the uncertainty of the author's future. The reflections shared in the first book, *Miss Your Forever*, were a testament to the love shared between two people, and the words provided validation and comfort to anyone who has been through a tragic loss.

—Kathy D.

Just finished your second book, *In a Heartbeat*. How beautifully written. The love you have for your wife is so sincere and so loving in every word you wrote. I cried and smiled at the same time. Remember that Sue will always be in your heart.

—Sheila L.

To anyone who is struggling with loss or grief, I must recommend two books that I have read. They are *In a Heartbeat* and *Miss Your Forever*. Both were written by a college friend of mine. Dom lost his wife, also someone I knew, suddenly and tragically. Although all my personal losses have not been recent, I found so much through reading these books that have helped me to address.

—Liz S.

I am currently reading a book by my friend Dominic Murgido called *In a Heartbeat: A Tale of Reflection, Faith, Hope, and Resilience: A Memoir.* It is Dom's second book written after the untimely and tragic death of his beloved wife more than ten years ago. His first book, *Miss Your Forever*, is an incredible look into his life after her death. Thank you, Dominic, for sharing these uplifting messages with us. When we can come to our path of grief, when we begin to slowly look up from the fog, it is beneficial to hear about the way others have begun to move toward a new beginning.

—Sylvia H.

Always a thoughtful and sharp professor that I had the distinct pleasure of being taught by. To be able to help others cope and somehow manage their grief while working through your own unimaginable pain is a testament to who you've always been: a man with great character, integrity, and resilience.

—Ryan M.

I highly recommend two books authored by Dominic Murgido: *In a Heartbeat* and *Miss Your Forever*. Both are incredibly honest, inspiring, validating, encouraging, and heartfelt. For anyone who has suffered loss (and who hasn't?), these writings bear witness to a beautiful love story, a courageous sharing of pain and sorrow, and also tools for adjusting to change, the value of forgiveness, and the assurance that life does go on. Your work honors your writing, it honors Sue, and it honors grief support in general.

—Anne N.

A heartfelt memoir that provides an inspiring message with honesty.
—Melissa R.

A meaningful story that allows you to ride along with someone's grief over the course of time. The selections of short topics after chapters were particularly interesting. The inclusion of entries from his journal placed you inside his head at the time he wrote them, further identifying the many things one thinks about while dealing with the loss of a spouse.

—John W.

Contents

Preface..xiii

Continued...xv

The Day That Changed My Life......................................1

Generally Speaking..3

Life Change 1...7

    Review of life change 1......................................14

    Reflections 15

Life Change 2...37

    Review of life change 2......................................44

    Reflections 45

Life Change 3...64

    Review of life change 3......................................70

    Reflections 72

Down the Rabbit Hole...93

Afterword...95

Acknowledgments...97

Preface

All of us who have had a loved one die must deal with the aftermath of that death. How we decide to deal with it can be the foundation of our future moving forward. The first death I remember was that of my grandmother followed by my grandfather six years later, both on my father's side.

Most of the other deaths I experienced were those who were friends of my parents. After college and my world expanded to include my wife and her family, more deaths were dealt with, including my wife's grandparents, her father, and her sister. My father died four months after my wife's sister. Approximately two months later, my wife died as a result of a vehicular accident. Her death changed everything in my life and how I look at death now.

It has been more than a decade and a half since my wife died, and I continue living my life with loss. Living (your life) with loss is not as bad as it sounds once you learn to live with your loss. All of us live with loss and are doing this without thinking about it or defining it. It is just life continuing on with you at the center and each day following the previous day in succession.

Living with loss may also include all past losses you experienced as being part of your life. Much depends on how long ago the death was as well as the relationship that existed between you and the deceased. Another factor is your age when the death occurs and the length of the relationship you had with your loved one.

Learning to live with loss through processing grief the right way can be challenging to do on your own. I recommend grief counselors, therapists, and support groups to help direct you along your grief journey. Without those tools, I would not have made it. With the help of those resources, I was able to discover practices that enabled me to cope with the heartache I was dealing with from an incomprehensible loss.

What you are about to embark on are my thoughts and experience of grieving as I look back at three life changes (stages / time periods) of my life that made an impact worth sharing with you. These periods of time when a change occurred placed me in a transitional phase of my life and is what happened personally to me.

I realized that with each life change, I was leaving a comfort zone. We are all familiar with comfort zones so much that many times, being within a comfort zone may prevent us from making choices due to being afraid to change because we are, well, comfortable. By not leaving a comfort zone, we may become complacent and stalled in life.

Leaving a comfort zone puts us in a place of the unknown—a place of uncertainty, risk, change—a new environment of physicality and mentality. I have realized, as you will read, that if I never had the courage to leave the comfort zones that became part of my life, the ability for transformation and growth would be nonexistent. As each transition occurred, it placed me in another life experience to allow additional choices to be made and risks taken as I moved forward.

I think every one of us who grieves goes through life changes at different times during our grief journey that intersects with our continuing lives. None of us have the same circumstances, so our changes will be totally different from each other. And most of us will not even recognize the life change when it is happening. We will continue on not knowing that we just crossed an invisible line that puts us in another place, a place that is hopefully better than where we have been.

It is only through journaling, writing reflections, and looking back that I recognized the changes that I personally went through, the causation of the changes, and the results that transformed me into another person in another chapter in this new life of mine.

Continued

Okay, so where was I? Oh, yes. It was the end of 2019. I had retired from a second short-lived career. I have signed up for social security early, and the plan was to enjoy life the best I can. I was delighted to move along at a pace that was my own. This was an opportunity for me to really think about my life and life in general.

Within this grieving process, there is so much that is happening to us mentally and physically that we aren't even aware of, nor do we think about changes in our lifestyle. Some changes just happen, and we are right there dealing with it while other changes can be planned.

Not being employed by choice was a sense of freedom. Never being retired before, I wasn't sure what to expect about how my time would be spent. Years ago, I was under the assumption that retirement meant time would continue to be enjoyed with my wife who would also be retired. Unfortunately, my wife's sudden, unexpected death had me retiring alone, something I wasn't prepared to do. I also wasn't ready to spend the last seventeen-plus years without her love.

My life since her death has been more or less documented in journals expressing my thoughts, observations, and memories about this grief journey that I have been on since the day that she died, a grief journey like no other and one that I could not have survived as well as I did without the unconditional love and companionship of my dog Hal.

Oh, and about those thoughts, observations, and memories, well, they became short passages of my writing I'll call reflections that appeared in various grief support newsletters and eventually in my own grief support newsletter I created to supplement a monthly grief support group I founded called *sudSSpirit*. It's an acronym for *sudden unexpected death of a Spouse Survivors in participation to inform, renew, improve, and triumph.* The support group, as well as the newsletters, became a resource for many people who were trying to find their way through the grieving process toward some sense of normalcy.

Some background is needed to bring you up to speed if this is the first time you picked up a book of mine. Let's review briefly what brought me to this point.

The Day That Changed My Life

It was the third Monday of a new year. It was Martin Luther King Jr. Day. It was January 16, 2006. And like any other day, it began the same and continued on its course in a familiar way.

I left for work after a goodbye kiss with my wife, Sue, and she more than likely followed suit in her routine of planning her morning of errands including a walk with her best friend Hal, our Blue Merle Sheltie on a wooded trail near the house. She wasn't due at work till 2:00 p.m. that day.

I was in a meeting at work all morning and by early afternoon was in my office when the phone rang. On the other end was her boss, owner of a local pharmacy where Sue worked as a pharmacy technician. He called to ask about Sue. She had not come into work, and his efforts to reach her were coming up empty. We had a brief conversation concluding that she must have gotten ill and is not picking up the home phone or her cell phone.

I told him I would get back to him and left work to go home to check on Sue. At home, all was well as it should be. Her car was gone, and the house was locked, and our dog Hal was there being Hal. I then surmised that she probably was on her way to work and had car trouble and probably had no cell service to seek help. I thought I would take the route she takes to work to find her, a route I never knew about until her birthday three days ago when she showed me a different way home from our day out together using the reverse of her usual route to work.

I came across a fire policeman ahead who was redirecting traffic. As I pulled up to him and rolled my window down, I asked what was happening. He told me there had been an accident with a fatality.

I broke down in tears just knowing that the fatality was my wife. I don't know how or why I instinctually knew this, but it was to be confirmed in the next few minutes.

After he called someone on his radio, I was asked to proceed ahead. Shortly down the road was an accident scene that was to haunt me for many years: fire trucks, ambulances, police vehicles everywhere; traffic cones, glowing flares, caution tape, flashing lights, and scores of first responders all over the intersection. The sight and sounds around me were one of disruption, chaos, fear, and uncertainty. I was alone even though surrounded by dozens of people I never met.

The looks on their faces immediately told me the story I did not want to hear. My life, as I loved it and knew it, was about to change forever, and there was nothing I could do to prevent it. After hearing the news directly from a police officer, I crumpled to the ground as a lost soul in a world I was no longer familiar with.

Generally Speaking

Someone just died. Depending on your relationship with them, the world you knew may change forever. And their death could have been expected or sudden. Either way, it is hurtful, heart-wrenching, and forever. You are immediately not present in a world you were part of just moments ago. You're physically present, but your mind is elsewhere.

You're in shock! You don't know what to do or where to go. You just want to stay right where you are, frozen in space and time with what thoughts that are managing to come to mind about the unknown you are now facing. You may crawl inside your being, saying nothing and staring into space. You may scream or cry, and there may be a physical weakness to your body or to your stomach. If you are alone, there will be a silence that cannot be defined after you scream out loud to no one, or if you remain silent, you may not be able to tell the difference between the usual silence and the silence that comes when tragedy strikes. But if you are alone, don't be. Call someone. Go somewhere. Don't be alone with this kind of news and heartache.

You are in a vulnerable position right now. You are not thinking straight. In a short time, your thoughts could go places they shouldn't. You need a trusted friend or family near you right then and now. Start talking, crying, keeping hydrated. You are not able to take care of your own needs at this very moment, so don't try to. There are others around you who will be there to assist in your basic necessities. Those others could include first responders, nurses, friends, coworkers, neighbors, family, or even a caring and compassionate stranger.

Once you cross the threshold of twelve to eighteen hours since finding out about their death, things will quiet down a little within you. This will be a good sign. People will still be around you who care for you and will help direct you to what immediate needs must be met. In some ways, they will be thinking for you and about you during this most stressful time of your life. This can be overwhelming if you start thinking into the future too far. Just don't.

After a sleepless night, exhaustion will settle in, as will disorientation. You will be on automatic pilot as you cater to the needs at the moment. Arrangements for the service will take place with as little or as much as you want to be involved in. For myself, I could not be part of any speaking publicly. I was lucky to be standing upright and somewhat coherent. Perhaps the sudden death aspect placed me in this position because I felt I was still in that shock mode and couldn't believe where my life was right now or where it was heading. But everyone is different in how they react depending on the circumstance.

After the day of the service, you are still in a whirlwind, not sure of anything or what comes next. This may be the only time you have to really let yourself grieve through tears. Give yourself time to do absolutely nothing but grieve for your loss of your loved one. Don't ignore this important task for yourself. Hopefully, you will have a few more bereavement days left from your employer. I would suggest taking more time if you have vacation days or any time that is owed to you. You need this extra time off away from the real world before you think about the return to work.

Upon entering the real world, everything changes. The smallest detail will be different. How you look at things will be different. How people treat you will be different. This will be a process that you will eventually get used to. I had a great employer to go back to. They allowed me the time to ease back into my position with my responsibilities. They understood the need I had for space around me and provided me with that space and understanding.

Not all employers or people you work with will be this way. If you have to go to your car on break to cry, do it. If it's possible to go home for lunch where you'll feel safer, do it. Don't be afraid to decline lunch invitations if you are not up to it. It is okay to say no to any suggestion or offer that you are not ready to do or may not be comfortable for you.

You will slowly get back to some sense of normalcy. For some, it is the return to work, and with that brings its own adjustments for you and those who work around you. For others, it is continuing on in a silent home or apartment being alone for the first time from many years of companionship. Whatever the return may be, you lost your way because you now feel compelled to continue on in the same manner that you have always done but this time without your spouse or loved one. It brings on a new dimension to life, a dimension of loneliness and confusion that no one wants to be in. You feel locked into this new life at times with no way out.

This is all part of getting back into the swing of things with living—living without them. You begin a new daily routine as it applies to your work world and your private world. If you feel the need or just know you cannot do this alone, please seek out a support group or a therapist. Start building a new kind of normal for yourself, knowing that you are really in control, and you can change things anytime you want to. Your goal is to get back to some kind of routine as that applies to your new situation. Things will never be the way they once were. Don't think too far ahead for your future. No need for any big decisions to be made unless some outside source is prompting you. Moving forward is something that *you* define.

As anyone who has lost a spouse can attest, death of an intimate changes everything. *Change* is a big word to use, but this word describes how you go from point A to point B. And if things need further development, change happens again from point B to point C. And this may continue for some time. It all depends on your situation and needs.

You and only you control change in your life. Not everyone needs change or even desires change. Your grief is your own thing and is very individual in its needs. How I look at change and how change happened for me may be totally not happening for you. Your journey may be very different, and yours may not have included all the miles I put on with mine. We are all different in how we deal with our grief, and our needs will be different because our situations are all different.

Many factors contribute to how we each deal with our grief: our age; the relationship we had with our loved one; how long we were with them; the circumstance surrounding the death, where they died; our family, faith, friends; our work status; our own health, guilt, regret, anger, denial, attitude. It can be a mix of all of these things that determine just how we will come to be during this next chapter of our life.

Sometimes, what may seem unimportant at the moment could be life-changing in the years ahead. It is my hope that my sharing of what I had to do to become a better me will inspire you to become a better you.

Life Change 1

My first year without my wife, Sue, was challenging and formidable. Her death was in the middle of January just two weeks into the new year. Neither of us knew that the previous twelve months would be our last full year of time together. As I look back at every measure of time that has passed from holidays and seasons to birthdays and anniversaries, I didn't know any of that would be the last time a memory would be made with her.

Continuing on without her was painful. I am grateful that I had the support of my daughter and sister during those beginning years, providing me with the love and encouragement I needed to become adjusted in this new world without my soulmate.

I believe that my wife's desire to obtain another dog three years before her death was a hidden miracle of sorts. This new puppy of four months that came from Ohio was exactly what she needed to complete a void after the departure of our daughter to college. This dog's birthday was Halloween, and Sue named him Hal. An intelligent Blue Merle Shetland sheepdog became our new family member in our household.

Sue had high hopes for Hal. She began training him, at once enrolling Hal in courses for good behavior such as puppy school and a Canine Good Citizen curriculum. She worked closely with Hal around our home and in our backyard as well as walks along many trails and among people along sidewalks of shopping centers, testing and training with verbal calls and hand signals.

Eventually, Hal and she became certified as a therapy team, an accomplishment in itself after a rigorous training program and qualifying for two different associations. They did not let that training go to waste and were out and about visiting nursing homes, assisted living facilities, institutions, hospitals, and were even a part of a therapy dog group where they would attend events with other therapy dogs and their handlers. Together, they helped others cope with their struggles, illness, and adversity, bringing support and a smile to their faces. After Sue's death, Hal became an important part of my life and my personal therapy dog.

Grieving is a slow process and one that cannot be rushed. Just when you think you are getting further along, another wave of grief strikes you out of nowhere. As years went by, I was becoming restless with what I was doing in my career as well as my part-time teaching at a local university. I was beginning to feel like I no longer belonged because of Sue's absence in my life.

In some regards, I felt stuck or stranded within myself and will never get better unless a change happened. The problem with that thought was I didn't know what to do about it. At the same time, I often reflected about the horrific accident that killed her as well as the careless driver who was responsible. Being where I lived and where I worked seemed to keep me focused on that event that made my life turn upside down.

With Hal by my side, I did feel confident that whatever I needed to do, he would be there to support me and be the comfort I needed while I was doing it. Besides the help of Hal, family, and some close friends, I also attended therapy as well as grief support groups for years. It was apparent once I began going to these how much I really needed them and how they became a lifeline for me to decide who I was now and where I was heading with my life.

After four years, it was time for a change and to leave a familiar comfort zone. This is one risk that I would be doing on my own (without Sue) for the first time. As crazy as this sounds, having Hal with me made me feel confident that I can do this. I decided to retire from an almost thirty-year career, sell the house that Sue and I spent thirteen years in, move to another state, and start a small business. A big decision with risks, but staying where I was just wasn't working for me.

Was I afraid? Absolutely! But I knew in my heart I had to do something different where I could make the best of it and be confident in my actions. I also felt that there was something gnawing at me from within that I just couldn't identify. I needed to work on that once I figured out what that was.

The plan came together, and I became a resident of a small town in the state of Vermont. My daughter lived a few hours from me in New Hampshire. My house was at the base of the towering Green Mountains with the Appalachian Trail nearby. As a small business owner, I also became involved with the local chamber of commerce. I realized that being totally removed from my past environment and now in a new setting was just what I needed.

Hal and I were now part of a community that we never have been before. As I was getting used to being a hands-on business owner in a new state, he was getting use to a new home, neighborhood, and backyard. This move allowed me to do something different and new and at times took me into unknown territory where I learned a lot about myself with the new friends I was making. I did not have triggers around me that were negative or put me in a sad place. I needed that kind of reprieve so that I can continue to move forward. Believe me, I was still grieving the loss of Sue but in a healthier way.

I sought out and attended a local grief support group as well as a therapist. Eventually, I started a local chapter of my support group *sudSSpirit* for the sudden unexpected death of a spouse or significant other. The original chapter was founded years prior in Pennsylvania and was still active with a good friend and facilitator taking over when I moved.

I located a new veterinarian and groomer for Hal, and we started to explore local trails around us in the woods as well as some local parks. A walk throughout the neighborhood always brought joy to Hal as he was able to meet our new neighbors and their dogs who came out to greet him. Hal eventually made new dog friends and became the king of our backyard. Hal was always on patrol for the black squirrels that were so prevalent in our tree line that bordered our property.

This change provided me with perspective in ways I could not have found should I have stayed where I was. I worked on my grief as I continued living in this new setting. Through my own meditation and prayer, I was starting to understand more of who I was at this very moment. I began to live *in the present* and really analyze my situation. Through the efforts of a therapist and a support group I was attending regularly, some revelations came to mind. There were far too many times that I would spend being angry and felt hate toward the driver who carelessly killed my wife and turned my world upside down.

I was now just starting to realize something about myself that I have been haunted with since the day my wife died. What I didn't know was that since the accident that took my wife away from me, I was harboring actual hatred toward the driver of that tractor trailer. I am not proud to admit the feelings of hate toward the person who was driving the truck that day. *Webster* defines *hate* as intense hostility and aversion usually deriving from fear, anger, or sense of injury. He took someone I loved away from me, my daughter, and countless other friends and family through his own negligence and carelessness.

I know *hate* is a strong word, but I have strong feelings surrounding it. I have been carrying this with me for over five years, and it continued to control me. These feelings are holding me back from moving forward. I know that now. Getting past this through any kind of resolution will be a difficult road ahead. I must work on this problem because hate is something that has never been part of my life before, and I don't want it to be now. All of this, with the resurgence of my grief and my realization of the hatred for the truck driver I've been carrying with me and not really knowing it, is really adding up to a perfect storm within me.

Now that I identified the problem of hate that was burning within me, I needed to devote time toward the solution of forgiveness. Being angry and spending my time with that emotion are not helping my personal mental health. Staying angry will not change the outcome, except to prevent me from moving forward in some capacity. I can't let this keep me back any longer.

After much prayer, meditation, and many sleepless nights thinking about this, I decided to put my heart into forgiving the driver. I realized that in order for me to move forward, I had to reach deep down within my soul and forgive the driver who took my wife away from me. I actually started thinking of him in a whole new light, wondering how he was coping with his actions of accidentally taking another life. Was he at the same job? Was he seeking therapy? I will forgive this man, whom I had never met, of his negligent and careless act of driving unsafely, speeding, running a red light, and striking the vehicle driven by wife and killing her instantly.

And forgiving is not just something that you just do. You have to believe in yourself and your true feelings, and you have to want to do it. Holding on to anger and distaste keeps you angry and depressed about what happened to your loved one and concentrating on that all the time prevent you from living again. I never thought I would forgive, but I realized how not forgiving was destroying who I am and who I wanted to be. I did not like that I was angry and resentful to the world.

I started to understand that being that way was keeping me stalled in life's path. I needed to move forward and become free again to do and choose what I wanted. Staying angry kept me confined and uncomfortable with myself and the world around me. You will feel better and more at ease to move forward. You will look at life through the eyes of hope instead of despair. You can begin to move forward and become whole again while rebuilding your life.

Not forgiving breeds anger, hostility, and hatred. Being angry and not forgiving allow you to continue living in the past and not being current to the present day. You don't even know that you are angry and are filled with hatred because it is so much inside you and part of your being. You just know you are not yourself, and it hurts and you see so much of life around you in a depressed and sad way. It's not an easy task to forgive. As C. S. Lewis once said, "Everyone says that forgiveness is a lovely idea until they have something to forgive." It took me until now to forgive the one person responsible for my wife's death. I now reflect on the time I wasted not forgiving.

This is a big step for me, a step I didn't even realize was needed until my relocation many years later. I am not sure had I never made this move, would I ever realize how angry and full of hate I was. Being so close to my familiarity and with the local anxieties and triggers that kept me in that frame of mind, I may have continued on in the state of mind of hate. That thought alone frightens me. Changing my environment helped me change my focus and made me see life from outside of the box I was trapped in.

I must give credit to my therapist at the time, who allowed me to talk things out and was able to help me discover what I was missing and conclude that forgiveness was one of the answers to my healing. This could be the thing that was gnawing at me that I could not identify. The need for recognition and the acceptance of forgiveness. This process provided me with the opportunity, and I decided to initiate the process, not a small task but accomplished, nonetheless. Forgiveness allowed me to live again without the burden of the past holding me back. Forgiving gave me hope. Hope is the magnetic force that pulls us forward. Hope is a lifeline.

After I was able to come to terms with forgiveness, I continued on with the small business and was hoping that this would fulfill my need to be part of something outside of the world I came from and on my own. About twice a month, I would see my daughter, and that was always a highlight for me and Hal. And Hal was getting accustomed to his new environment and liked the parks and trails nearby for his walks.

Sales for the business were average. There were some days that they were better, but that didn't happen often enough to increase cash flow and savings. Then during the second year, there were multiple equipment failures that drained my financial nest egg along with a tropical storm, whose strength took its toll on the community with major flooding, eliminating fall foliage tourist season, and reduced water pressure for weeks. Sales plummeted, and I was beginning to weigh my options as to my next move. I had finances to keep going, but if it didn't turn around, what I had would be gone, and that would put myself in financial jeopardy.

I decided to close the business. This decision was hurtful in many ways. I really enjoyed the customer interaction. I learned how to roast coffee beans, a new skill that I became very good at. It was fun to be part of a community as a small business owner. I sold off everything, but the coffee roaster and relocated that to my garage where I put the business online. I also started to look for employment in the area, particularly teaching at a local college. During this time, I was still facilitating my support group locally, attending another support group for myself, and also seeing a therapist. There was a lot to think about with regard to the direction my life would be taking eventually.

I was enjoying all this extra time I got to be with Hal, spoiling him as much as I could. I sold coffee online to past customers of the shop and was able to take in more of the beauty of the mountains that surrounded me in all the seasons. After a full year, it was becoming apparent that my coffee sales were slowing down, and the job search was not producing any opportunity for teaching. I thought that I could roast my coffee from anywhere. It didn't have to be where I was, so I began to think about moving back to Pennsylvania and bringing the roaster with me. I also thought that teaching opportunities may be more prevalent back home.

I also believed that since I was able to *forgive* during my time away, the return to my home state would be more satisfying to my current mindset of emotions, and I'd be able to handle life with better confidence than I did before. Just maybe that was the underlying reason for my decision to close the business and move back.

Another decision and risk to be taken and life change. Now I'm selling a home I've only had for three years—and then, of course, another relocation but a move back to familiar territory. I started planning this out with long one-sided talks to Hal about this relocation. I got the vibe from Hal that he was happy wherever I went as long as he had access to a nice yard.

Review of life change 1

Everything I did was *on my own* for the first time: leaving a career, selling a home, relocating, buying a home, buying and operating a small business, starting a second support group, learning a new skill like roasting coffee, forgiving, selling a business, selling a home, relocating again. From the time life change 1 began till it was transitioning to life change 2, many years went by, adding to the new experience of my search for purpose and fulfillment. While I was leaving one comfort zone and beginning a new one, I was getting stronger in my faith of making it.

Reflections

I thought we were going to grow old together

I wish I had a dollar for every time I heard this mentioned among those of us who grieve the loss of a spouse. We all believed that, and why shouldn't we? Life is grand for us in a relationship that is filled with love and companionship. No matter how much or how little amount of time we shared with one another, life was good.

Our partner is diagnosed with a terminal illness. They become very sick very fast. They sustain an injury that becomes life-threatening. Our soulmate has a heart attack, a stroke, an aneurism. They have an accident at work or while they are enjoying a favorite sport or pastime. Our significant other is killed while on a boat or by a train or in a plane crash. They are killed in a vehicle accident or drown or even murdered.

However it happens, they are gone. Life as we knew it is gone with them, for it will never be the way it was from now on. We were comfortable with our partner and our lives together. We did not see this coming. No one did.

There was so much more that we wanted to do together, share with one another: travel, explore new adventures, dine out more, visit friends and family more frequently, take extended weekends, and grow old together. None of that can happen with them anymore. We are shocked and somewhat traumatized by this life-changing event that in some cases happened in the blink of an eye, while in other cases, death lingered on for some time.

Regardless of the circumstances, we now begin another part of our life but not before we accept the reality of the grief that we feel and the emotional experience that won't go away. Our grief journey begins here. This journey is not one to take too lightly. It will be difficult at times, and you cannot do this alone. Support from family, friends, counselors, and bereavement support groups may be needed and are there for you to gain a sense of healing and balance within your life.

After months, maybe years, you will begin to feel better as time marches on. Our loss will eventually not dominate our thoughts, and we will have many past memories to reflect upon as we look forward to our future. Although we are alone now minus our better half, their presence is with us spiritually, helping and guiding us through many tomorrows as we learn to live once again in a world full of hope and promise.

Stop asking why

Those of us who have lost a loved one are familiar with the sudden unexplainable feelings of sadness and loneliness that we can feel in an instant, out of the blue, without any kind of warning or preparedness that it is about to happen. And it doesn't matter where we are or what we are doing. It is present and affecting us, and it is all so real.

These occurrences happen very often in the beginning of the grief journey, and with them happening so close to the loss, we could understand that it is happening and really don't question why. It continues throughout the first year, and as most of us can attest to, friends, coworkers, relatives all say the same thing: "It takes a good year to get over it."

I am sure you were shaken at those words as I have been. Most of those who never have been through a loss such as ours have no clue, and a year is not the marker that any of us should think that we will be healed, like turning off a light switch. It's not that easy.

The second and third year come, and these occurrences continue. However, they come less, and the duration of the sadness is shorter. During this time, we will start to question our own healing process and wonder if something is wrong with us. What we are experiencing is okay, and there is nothing wrong with us.

Time moves on, and we carry on in our lives missing our loved one but realizing that we have to move forward in order to heal and get better with our lives. And then those feelings of sadness come again to us, and this time, we are concerned and also question why. We will take time to analyze why. We may lose sleep over why. We may get sick over why. We will spend many hours, if not days, wondering why, but there are no answers to this question.

It still happens to me. It just did recently out of the blue, no warning, in an instant. I was spiraling down into sadness and loneliness right after having a pleasant evening at home watching a good movie. It came and went, and by the next morning, I was okay again.

I stopped asking why. There are no answers to this question. I started accepting the fact that this will happen on occasion, and that it is okay. It is part of the big picture of the grief journey that I am on. It does not come as often anymore, and it may eventually stop coming altogether. But I don't know, and I am not going to worry about it one way or the other. *Acceptance* should become part of your vocabulary. Be patient with yourself, and certainly don't expect more than what you can handle at the present time.

Rediscovering the new you

Losing your spouse or significant other is painful, very painful. Any loss comes with much anxiety, sleeplessness, uncertainty, shock, trauma, and the realization that your world as you knew it ceases to exist. It is you, alone, and any reference to your better half or to you as being part of a couple is gone, long gone.

Friends and even family members look at you so much more differently than ever before. There is a sense of discomfort with you around. No one knows how to act or what to say around you, and it is okay. You didn't know how to act or what to say around those who you knew who lost someone close to them. Our society isn't good at knowing how to deal with others who lose a loved one. It's not exactly something that is "gone over" in our development as people or in any education process. I believe we need to work on that.

All of the stages and phases of grief that have been talked about, written about, researched about are all clear and defined. We read about them, share them with others going through the same thing we are going through in support groups or in a one-to-one counseling session with a trained professional. And that is all good and understood, but sometimes, everyone's phase or stage isn't exactly like what they say or what one goes through. That is okay. Realize that each one of us is going to go through this journey in our own way on our own time schedule. Knowing this and accepting it will help you in many ways so that you don't feel like you are alone out there and isolated from others.

The benefit of support groups is that at times, those who are in attendance are at these different phases of their grief compared to you and to the others, and that can be very helpful. Listening and sharing amongst each other allow everyone to learn from each other and feel a little bit better about where they are on their journey. This is a healthy feeling when you realize that someday, you may feel better than you do right at that moment because others who have been there have survived it, and they are there to prove it and talk about it.

It may take a long time, a substantial time to rediscover who you now are, and at times, this discovery happens in small increments over a period of time. So if you think once you discover something new about the new you, just wait because there will be something else that will be coming along at another time. This is a process that seems to not end as we think it might, at least that is what I am experiencing. I am still discovering and finding out many things about myself as I make this journey.

I have been through and have put myself through many changes and challenges in my life without her, and all of it was worth it. The good, the bad, the indifferent, the successes as well as those things that just didn't work out the way I thought they would, but I tried and became a better person for trying and certainly have learned a lot about me along the way. You know what they say; when life gives you lemons, make lemonade. Turn a negative into a positive for yourself and others.

All of us who are going through this grief journey face challenges. We may not think of them as challenges and changes as they are happening, but afterward, we realize that we overcame it and got through it. Facing situations alone for the first time can be very difficult. Those *first times* don't all come within that first year either, contrary to what most people outside of our grief world believe or have read about from people who have not been through this.

Firsts can be as simple as grocery shopping alone and for one to a more complicated and complex situation like moving out of your house that you shared for many years. The birthdays, date-of-death days, anniversaries, season changes—they all factor into rediscovering the new you. Changing careers, retiring, beginning a new job that you didn't have to have before but is now a necessity—they all factor into rediscovering the new you. Changing your diet, health concerns, new socialization circles, learning to do things you'd never thought you had to worry about—they all factor into rediscovering the new you.

And it is okay. You can do this. You have to believe in yourself and have faith and hope that better days are ahead, and they truly are for you. Stay confident and focused, and learn to accept the new person that you are becoming, a person who looks forward to new experiences, enjoying life, and laughing again.

My favorite chair

It was an evening around sunset, and I just reentered the house after playing with my dog out in the backyard. I sat in my favorite chair that I recently had reupholstered. The chair is in my family room, and while sitting there at sunset, I was able to watch the sun slowly go down in between the branches of the trees in my backyard with my dog Hal at my feet. I enjoy the feeling of this chair, and now with its new look, it felt even better. Sitting on this chair has always provided me with comfort and peace.

Let me tell you about this chair. My wife and I bought this chair on sale at a family-owned furniture store near our home at the time. We both liked the chair, which was a Flexsteel brand known for its durability and oak frame. It was comfortable and well-made, and it seemed to fit you just right as you sat down into its soft embrace with firm arm supports.

Through the years, furniture was bought and sold, but this chair stayed part of the family, perhaps more so by my own desire to hold on to it. Not sure how much attachment my wife had to it over the years. The dogs we owned also liked the chair to my dismay.

Throughout the years since my wife died, I have been through many life changes and challenges, some I instituted while others just happened. We all go through life's journey in different ways and experience the triumphs and tragedies. With my relocation, many things that were possessed did not make the cut to come with me, and some of the things that did come eventually found a new home elsewhere with someone else. My favorite chair remained, and I thought it would be time to give it a new look.

I found a local upholsterer who said that he could do it, and it would be less expensive if I found material he had in stock that I liked. I wanted to find a blue pattern for the chair, and his selection for blues was limited to one, but this blue pattern was a winner in my book. In fact, the only blue he had was the same kind of material that was currently on my chair. It was material used for Flexsteel furniture products, but instead of the tan pattern it now had, it was done in a blue and had a flower design that almost matched the current pattern. What are the odds of not only picking this upholsterer but his having only one blue color that I liked and its being the same fabric used on this kind of chair from the manufacturer? I guess things happen for a reason. He did the chair in two days for a great price. My wife would have been proud of me getting such a great deal.

I began to reflect about the chair as I sat in it as the sun was setting. Do I like the chair for its never-ending comfort, or as I now realize, do I like the chair because it is the last piece of upholstered furniture I own that I bought with my wife? Or is there something else that draws me to the significance of this chair?

The chair was purchased at that family-owned furniture store I mentioned earlier. The location of that furniture store is the same location of the intersection where my wife died in a fatal vehicle accident just over seven years ago. Inside that furniture store is where I learned of the life-changing news and collapsed in anguish to the floor in the middle of caring first responders.

Many years ago, I was standing in this store on a happy occasion, purchasing a chair with my wife, and now I am in a heap of crumbled humanity, trying to make sense of an unexpected death of my soulmate. What are the odds of this store location being the common denominator of two events in my life (one happy, one tragic) separated by many years? I never thought about this chair in that regard until now. I guess things do happen for a reason.

Giving the chair a face-lift allowed me to give my life new meaning, new direction, moving forward but retaining the comfort and peace of a life once past, a life that was shared by two who bought a chair together and now a chair enjoyed by one. The chair is more than a piece of furniture. It tells a story and brings back some nice memories and in an important way, connects to life's triumphs and tragedies and remains a meaningful presence in my new world.

I will always keep this chair. It was once a part of us and now is part of me. The chair symbolizes a safe place to be, to relax, to read, to nap, to meditate, and to watch a sunset on any evening anywhere I live.

Does anybody really know how we feel?

As I continue with my life without my wife, I see changes in my world. My world has been so very different since her passing. Some of the traditions I am still trying to hold on to, while others have been stopped or soon will be stopped. It's hard to hold on to something that only mattered when there were two of you who enjoyed it. When there is one of you left, the fun goes away. Each year is different in its purpose to me. The purpose is for me trying to understand and accept life that is so different than the many years I have spent with my wife.

These kinds of changes have to be looked upon as a positive in your life. You must recognize that you are ready to let go of some of the things while trying to build upon new things that matter to you. In your own way, at your own pace, you will find new things. It will never be the same as it once was, but it can be new to you, and it can become part of your new life without your loved one.

Some of us who go through this grieving process view the outside world differently now. There are times I don't want to have any part of it, and on weekends, I just want to stay indoors and watch it move on through my window. I am content with that, and that alone time allows me to reflect in my own private world of my house. I reflect through thoughts that are translated by pen and communicate to others only if I wish to. Other times, I feel like I need to be around people, even people I don't even know. I want to be part of their world and be in places they are in like parks, malls, restaurants, or events. Being around others at times supplies its own sense of belonging to me when I want to be a part of the outside world.

The people around us really don't know how we feel. Those who are neighbors, friends, coworkers, even family members just don't get it. They think that our grieving process can be compared to a bad cold or sore back, and in a few weeks, we will be good again.

They can't understand our confusion, tears, sensitivity, and sometimes our unwillingness to be part of their day. They question our emotional state and suggest that there must be something wrong with us that it is taking so long to get over it. *It*—imagine someone referring to us being robbed of our loved one way too early as an *it*?

There are people who really do know how we feel. Where do you find them? A grief support group. I am a firm believer in support groups, any kind of support groups that are existing to help those who are in need to become better at who they are or help to cope with a situation in their life, like the loss of a loved one.

Being part of a grief support group will allow you to express yourself to others and listen to others. This is such a great healing process because it provides you a sense of not being alone in your grief. Continued attendance in support groups builds a bridge that will allow you to slowly cross to the sunny side on your journey through this process. Being part of multiple bereavement support groups has helped me and continues to help me cope and stay focused with who I am and where I am going with my life.

If you are not part of one, I encourage you to do so. You have nothing to lose but some pain and heartache that you are feeling, and you will not be alone in your grief.

After you

I never dreamed that there would be an *after you*. There was a *before you*, and I remember that well because my life was missing something. Then you came along, and it became *we*. Both of us like the *we* that was created, and neither one of us thought of the possibility that the *we* would ever not be a *we*. No one thinks that. No one who is involved in a loving relationship thinks that or believes that it can happen. It is just not something to be thought of. Life happens, and time passes, and all the joys that you both share continue and become part of your lives and your memories together.

It happened to me as it did for so many people before me and so many more people yet to be. I lost a loved one. My wife died way too soon, and this tragedy was very difficult to deal with for many years, and I had to deal with *after you*.

What was now going to happen to me after you? What would my future be after you? How will I live again after you? How different will my life be after you? What am I going to do after you? Where will my life lead after you? Who am I now after you? Can I survive after you?

These are a few of the questions I pondered that needed answers, and you just can't consult a family member, a friend, a book, a website, or social media to find the answers. The answers to these questions about your destiny are within you. It will take time, patience, and reflection to find them.

There is life after the death of a loved one. It doesn't seem that way at first when your world is turned upside down, and you feel that there is no hope for you. Seeking help for you is an important step in the healing process. Many of us don't think we need this, but in reality, we all do. Look in the newspaper, search online, ask a friend, call a hospital, library, funeral home and inquire about a bereavement support group or a therapist or counselor to help you help yourself through this grief journey ahead of you. Just talking out loud about what you are going through and hearing your own words will make you feel better and allow those listening to know where you are in your journey and provide the comfort you need as you move forward.

Eventually, one step at a time, you will know what is going to happen to you. You will know your future and feel good about it. You will live again. You will understand the change in your life for yourself and those around you. You will see a new direction that your life will lead you to. You will become a new you using the inspiration, love, and encouragement that you gained from your loved one to move forward with your life and feel a new sense of purpose. You will be a survivor of this loss and in time will look back and reflect how far you have come. I have been able to acknowledge, adapt, and accept what has happened to me after you. Because of you, life matters after you.

Dogs can be a griever's friend

So much has been written about dogs and the role they play in our lives. Many people whom I have known had a dog at one time in their life. Many more always had a dog and continue to have a dog that shares their life with them and their family.

Man's best friend, a child's playmate, a companion to you—their role and function to us is countless, and that role is one of unconditional love and loyalty. They can't speak, but they know and realize all that is happening around them and in their own ways are able to provide comfort and a sense of peace to us when we need them too.

I had a dog growing up that was shared with my sister. After college and then marriage, a dog was destined to be part of my family. My wife always had a dog growing up and loved dogs as much as I did. When I look back at all the dogs we had in our home, they all played a significant role in that part of our lives that we were experiencing at the time.

Dogs were part of our marriage and the development of our family. Upon the arrival of our daughter, dogs continued to be part of our lives and hers. Children look at dogs so much differently than us adults, but they have their own place for them in their hearts.

Dogs love to be a part of whatever it is you are doing, whether you like that or not. They are loving and caring and love to have your attention and be talked to. They seem to know when we are happy or sad and act accordingly to celebrate with us or help us.

There is a special dog in my life. This dog is one that my wife selected, and we became owners of a Blue Merle Sheltie as a four-month-old puppy. My wife named him Hal. His birthday is on Halloween. Hal is adorable and very intelligent.

My wife and Hal became inseparable, and this dog did everything, went everywhere, and was always thought about in anything that was planned. My wife spent as much of her time with this dog as she could in many areas of adventure and experiences. Hal was put through many classes of instruction, being awarded with one completion certificate after another, including therapy dog training.

Hal seemed to really excel in therapy dog training, and my wife loved to take him to visit those less fortunate in nursing homes and assisted living facilities. Sometimes I wasn't sure who enjoyed bringing smiles to faces more, she or the dog. They were indeed a team in this venue and provided an extra dose of happiness to an otherwise drab day to the people in these elder care settings.

My wife's time with Hal was cut short when she died in a vehicle accident. She was only forty-eight; the dog was only three at the time. The hardest thing I ever had to deal with was the death of my wife. The second hardest was telling my daughter. The third was breaking the news to Hal. I remember walking into the house that day and being happily greeted by the dog, as usual. I dropped to the floor and hugged Hal while sobbing for what seemed like hours. He waited at the kitchen door that night for her to come home. Hal seemed depressed and sad and wasn't eating and spent most of his time in a corner. He needed closure, and my daughter and I had a thought. We called the funeral home and took Hal there to see my wife, his master. I would not believe it if I didn't see it, but after seeing her lifeless body lying there and no voice, movement, or touch was coming from her, Hal then realized that she wasn't coming home. It was a sight I shall never forget.

Dogs' emotions are no different than ours. He was saddened by the loss of his master and was in mourning for a while. We mourned together. We spent a lot of time next to each other. We cried and helped to provide comfort to one another.

Ironically, Hal became my therapy dog. I was now the one whom he was helping with his charm and personality, his presence and kindness, his gentleness and kisses. He was helping me through the most difficult period of my life. Life's challenges and changes can destroy us. Man's best friend has been there to help me and provide a comfort level that is indescribable. Hal has been a true friend and has helped me through my slow recovery from a life-altering situation.

Hal has helped me decide to retire from an almost-thirty-year career and adjust to the new me whom I didn't even know yet. He has helped me deal with my sadness and adjust to the loneliness over the years. Hal has helped me through all the *firsts* without her and the changing seasons with memories. And he is always up for "what's next" in our life together, just like my wife once was. Hal is always there supporting, encouraging, and loving unconditionally.

I am really not sure how I would have fared out in all of this *life* stuff had it not been for Hal. There has never been a dog like him before in my life, and I don't know if there ever will be again. He maintains a special place in my heart.

Hal is getting older, and signs of age are showing. I have to come to terms with the fact that he will leave me at one point to join his master, who left both of us many years ago. When that day comes, another life-altering situation will happen to me. We must recognize that the sun sets and rises daily, time moves on, life continues. We move forward and take steps toward a better and brighter tomorrow.

I love my dog Hal. He is responsible for helping me make it through my grief journey. I am grateful for his love, devotion, compassion, and presence in my life. Never underestimate the comfort of dogs.

Living with it

It comes as fast as an unpredictable thunderstorm and catches you completely off guard. It hurts your heart and brings numbness to your soul. Your eyes well up with tears, and you begin to cry. You feel empty, your heart aches, and you want to be alone right now.

Something brought it on, and you struggle to figure out what. Sometimes, you know, and sometimes you don't, and that's okay. But for whatever reason, you are experiencing an emotion connecting you to the loss of a loved one. This happens throughout the rest of your life, sometimes harder than other times, but there is a potential for it to happen to you anytime, anywhere. There is no stopping it or controlling it. It is now a part of you, and you have to learn to live with it.

Living with it can be challenging. You think that it should not happen after three, seven, or even ten years, but it does and may continue to follow you as you move forward with your life. Most people don't understand this unless they also have experienced this and have lost a loved one who was so much a part of their life. The love that we had for them never went away, and we continue to love them for being the person they were for us.

Some of us still feel their presence, say their name out loud when we are alone, talk with them as we lie in bed at night, seek advice and guidance about the life we now lead without them. They continue to be a part of our lives, living in our hearts and subconscious, and occupying our souls with their love for us. They want us to be happy and not to dwell on their passing and our loss of them.

Time passes, and over the years, it is hard not to be affected by a trigger of some kind that will bring back a memory of an event from the past you shared with them. It makes you miss them all over again, and at times, it feels like it just happened, even though time and reality tell us it was long ago.

> Time is an equal opportunity employer. All of
> us have exactly the same number of hours and
> minutes every day. Wealthy people can't buy

more time. Scientists can't invent new minutes.
And you can't save time to spend on another day.
(author unknown)

Using your time wisely and allowing yourself to experience the occasional thunderstorm knowing that there is a silver lining out there ahead of you make good sense. The harshness of your hurt will pass like the thunderstorm, and you will feel good again. Don't dwell on the whys and feel bad for yourself. You are not alone in this. It's all about living with it.

Silence

Silence is part of our lives. There are many places where we have to be silent or allow minimal sound, such as a library, a place of worship, a hospital, or a museum. Some people like it to be silent in their homes or in their cars while they drive.

We like the presence of silence after a full day with children or grandchildren or even a tough day at work. We look forward to silence at bedtime or when we are reading an interesting book. It seems much more silent after a fresh snowfall. Early in the morning, when taking a walk, it is more silent to us with less traffic in our neighborhood or on a trail in a wooded setting.

Silence can also be deafening and not liked by some of us. When we have lost a spouse, silence is very prominent in our lives. There are no more conversations with them, and just the lost sound of their voice is disturbing to us. We long to hear them talk again even though there were many times in the past we wanted them to stop talking. Now, we'd love to hear them just one more time.

Sometimes, not having someone else in the house or the apartment is too silent. The sound of silence with no movement by another person or knowing that no one else is with you where you live can be troubling. Silence dominates our lives where we no longer have anyone to share the daily mail with or the opinions we formed about the news of the day. We lack a partner to eat with, to go out with, and to nap with. In many respects, we have lost a social connection to the outside. Social silence can be difficult to deal with.

We have a choice to break the silence. We have the ability to make our lives become whole again in some small way. It will never be the way it was, but it can become better than how it is for you now.

One suggestion to break the silence can be music. Music can make you feel better about situations. I listen to many songs during the course of a day that make me smile or recall an event, a happy moment in my past, a feeling that I am thankful to have had my wife be part of my life. Watching a favorite movie that we shared together also helps me. Volunteering for a cause and helping others can be beneficial to break the silence while communicating with others in a role that will bring you a sense of peace.

Being part of a club or organization that has weekly or monthly meetings will allow less silence and more sharing of thoughts and ideas with others. Reaching out to family members and friends to have dinner with or attend an event with are also ways to break the silence for us.

Silence isn't always a bad thing for us. There is a place for it. I find silence comforting at times to reflect and write. Silence helps me clear my head of thoughts and concerns and allows me to let go of sadness through methods of meditation. There are times I look forward to a little silence to feel the presence of the love I still have for my wife.

You must be able to be the one in control of silence in your life. Whether you want it or not, it should be a choice, not a sentence. You must encourage yourself to break the silence when you need to or cherish the silence when you want to.

My discovery of journaling

If someone told me five years ago that I would journal someday, I would have looked at them like they were crazy. *Journaling* was something that did not appeal to me. Maybe it took a life-changing situation—like the sudden, unexpected death of my wife—for my opinion to change on this topic.

Within days of my wife's passing, I found myself jotting down thoughts, fears, emotions, anger, regret, and confusion on three-by-five index cards. Each day, I would complete two or three cards with expressions of pain, frustration, and loneliness. It is so common for those of us who have experienced the loss of a loved one to have feelings of hopelessness and helplessness. I found journaling to be a great release of my sadness and depression that I was experiencing with the knowledge that I was now without my wife. It also helped me with the struggle of so many unanswered questions concerning the rest of my life.

This daily ritual continued, and by the end of the first year, I completed about 250 cards. I received a journal of blank-lined pages from someone as a gift. It was at that time I realized I was journaling and did not even realize it through my unrefined methods of utilizing simple three-by-five index cards.

Sometimes I would write a single word or only a few words to express my feelings. Other times, I wrote incomplete sentences. Grammar, punctuation, and spelling did not matter when I wrote my thoughts and feelings. The content of what I was writing is what mattered. Depending on the time of year or the relevancy to a special date, there are many thoughts to reflect upon and write about. I date the entries and sometimes note the weather or a significant news item that is happening along with my thoughts. I reflect on things and how different it is without my wife being with me. I often comment on "how she would say this or ask that" if she were physically here with me or "how much I miss that about her."

My writings are not all sad. They also contain happy thoughts, memories, and even questions. There is something about writing down a question that makes it easier to deliberate the answer. And if you do not answer the question, it will be asked again on another day as you continue to write your thoughts. Eventually, you will answer it or resolve the conflict somehow.

I write daily, usually at the end of the day. I pick this time for the silence of the night and, in a way, as a ritualistic approach to going to bed alone, something that I am not used to doing. I find comfort in that time of day, pondering my thoughts and reducing my experiences to writing. I realize that putting my thoughts on paper allows me to vent, gives me a sense of peace, and provides me with an unofficial progress report at the same time.

Writings can be as simple as random thoughts jotted down that can become priceless months or years later as you process your experiences and feelings. I wrote for about a year and a half before I even thought about looking back at some of what I had already written in the past. I have never read all that I have written, nor do I go back regularly, just on occasion.

When you return to the past writings that you created, it allows you to see where you were and compare that to where you are now so that you can further understand where you are going. I read things that I wrote that I couldn't believe. It's amazing how you can believe in something at one time and have another viewpoint on the same thing a month or so later. I also read some parts that made me cry all over again or smile at my humility. This process of writing can bring tears. There is nothing healthier than a good cry as you grieve your loved one.

Whatever works for you is what you do. Some people are more comfortable with a keyboard when expressing thoughts as an electronic journal on a computer. I began on index cards and expanded to an organized, bound book form.

I continue to write with a pen on lined pages in a more traditional journal format. This form is best for me because it can be taken anywhere and be able to write anyplace. I find that when we think of things or experience an emotion as it relates to our bereavement, it is important to recognize it and jot it down. It may help us later or might mean something in the future as we continue to work through our grief journey.

When my wife died, my life and how I view the world has changed. This new world of mine is without her. I try to use my time of sorrow in order to grow as a new person through the journaling process. Journaling is for your benefit, and you can choose to keep it private to you. I encourage you to start and recognize how it can help you as it does for me.

Progress is something we all like to see in ourselves, especially in our own time of need. Our time of need combined with our grief experiences will yield with time. Be patient and allow yourself to heal.

Life Change 2

After great reflection and finishing what I had to do, it was time for me to move on to another chapter of my life. This time, I was in a better place emotionally than I ever had been, and it was from this past adventure that took me to another state where I took meaningful steps along the path to healing. I was guided by an inner voice, a gut feeling, or maybe my own consciousness. The guides that got me there were now taking me back to Pennsylvania.

I did not want to return to the same area where I lived before, so I began exploring towns nearby. Even though it's been like seven years by this time, I feared that I would be still experiencing negative triggers if I returned to live in the same area. One fear that has stayed with me no matter where I lived was vehicle-accident scenes. When I would drive past one or just observe one, a trigger would put me into an anxiety attack that made me an emotional wreck. It created a flashback in my mind to the accident scene where my wife was killed that I unfortunately discovered on my own. Although that fear can still happen regardless of where I live, being in another town would eliminate other negative triggers.

I found a nice home that would be good for me and Hal. Upon being settled, I was fortunate to be able to teach again part-time at the same university as before. I also returned to sudSSpirit's original chapter and became the facilitator after my three-year hiatus while dedicated friends kept it alive in my absence. I also had my coffee roaster installed and began to roast coffee and sell it to friends, family, and neighbors. I was welcomed back as a volunteer into organizations that I was part of before my departure. Hal loved his back and side yards and the many parks we found to take our walks.

Not sure how to explain my feelings or outlook at this time, but I had a sense of renewal, rebirth, and growth. The realization of my need to forgive and the forgiveness that I was able to accomplish made me whole again. This was the first time I was experiencing these feelings since Sue died. I felt comfortable where I was spiritually and emotionally. This second change or phase I was now in felt more relaxed than the first one. I also felt more in control of who I was. I can only assume that this outcome I was experiencing was the by-product of my three-year residence in Vermont and all that I gained from that experience. I can't imagine that remaining where I was—in Pennsylvania—would have had the same results. In fact, I think I would have been worse off with no signs of any kind of progress in my grief journey.

So what made me decide on doing change 1, and for that matter, how did I come up with the timing and the deciding on change 2? I believe in soul-searching and praying for help and guidance. I also believe that our loved ones only left us in the physical sense. They are present to us in the spiritual and emotional realm and do look after and guide us in our life without them. After many hours of thinking about this, I firmly believe I was guided (persuaded) to take action that would continue to help me through what I was going through at the time. Whether or not I decided to do it was up to me since I have free will, but in this matter, I decided for it not against it.

Part of experiencing change is to have the courage to want to move forward. Once that is achieved, it is a little bit easier to move forward. Along with courage is taking risks. Sometimes it takes longer than we want for us to be comfortable with taking risks as we try to improve ourselves. If you don't develop courage and take risks at some point through your journey, change will continue to be out of your reach, and you will miss out on living life.

Being back in Pennsylvania also brought *firsts* again. I've learned that firsts will always be there. Now the firsts I would be experiencing will be the firsts with a new home and location after my experiences in Vermont. Holidays, birthdays, anniversaries, seasons, and all of these firsts will also include Hal and how he now must get used to and experience new surroundings and be present to help and support me. My schedule was lighter in that I was teaching college part-time, and most times, it was evenings at two campus locations. I was home during the day with class preparation and being with Hal. I was also volunteering and roasting coffee.

After about two years of being in my new location and the fall season was approaching, I realized that the next year would mark the tenth year since Sue died, a milestone in some ways and hard to believe it has been that long. Thinking of her daily since her death has kept me close to her.

For the last ten years, I believe I have been suffering from a kind of PTSD whenever I observed a vehicle accident. This was as a result of my witnessing the horrific accident scene that my wife was involved in on the day of her death. Not knowing the reason she did not arrive at work that January afternoon, I decided to take the route she takes to work to discover the vehicle accident that she was killed in along with all the sights, sounds, and smells of a tragedy with a fatality. An image burned into my mind that shook me to the core at that time and still did to this day.

Ten years is a long time to have this issue, and before now, I wasn't ready with trying to deal with it or even consider how to solve it. In so many ways, if you are not ready and willing to take action on an issue or a problem, then you are wasting your time trying. It will never happen for you.

As the calendar page was going to flip over to January 2016, I decided that I wanted to do something about helping myself. This decision was well-thought-out during the last three months, and it was now or never to try to rid myself from those awful anxiety attacks and PTSD that I have been experiencing for the last ten years whenever I encountered any accident scene.

I have a good friend and decided to ask him for a favor. I wanted to ask if he would help me help myself and if he was available on this one particular Saturday in January. My objective was to revisit the scene of the accident at the intersection where my wife lost her life. I have not been back there since the day it happened ten years ago and to be frank, had no intention to do so, but the emotional trauma and stress that happens to me in a dream or when I come across any accident scenes since that day has just got to come to an end. Before this moment in time, I felt like I wasn't ready to do this. Now I am. I felt confident in myself after preparing for the last few weeks with meditation and prayer.

I selected the exact day of the accident and close to the time of when it occurred. I met my friend at a parking lot about five miles away from the intersection. From there, I would ride in his vehicle to the intersection, and we would park in a convenience store parking lot (if it is still there) that is at one of the corners. I needed to be present at this intersection that was in disarray ten years ago to one that was normal and functioning as it should be. I cautioned him that I didn't know how I would react that day, but I felt the need and the desire to try. Worse case, he may have to drive me for medical attention should I become distressed and experience a severe anxiety attack.

Upon arrival at the location, I took in the view and everything around it: buildings, businesses, traffic, people walking around. I walked around two corners of the intersection just observing the normal functioning of the intersection, hearing conversations of people and the sight and sound of traffic moving and stopping at the traffic signal. I watched as the scene in front of me had no trauma or sadness, no fatalities or closed roads, no flashing lights, no orange cones or caution tape, no emergency vehicles or uniformed first responders. I stood safely and took a deep breath and closed my eyes, capturing the moment. I experienced that intersection in a normal capacity for the first time in my mind's eye. I felt positive and comforted. I had an epiphany moment. I walked back to the car and joined my friend feeling like what I just experienced mattered to me.

It's never too late to try to better yourself with your grief journey. You will know when it is time to take another step. Trust your instincts. I knew I could never revisit that intersection until I was ready. It took me ten years to be ready, and doing this on the same day of the accident years later sealed the deal. This was a life-changing moment for me—facing my fear and succeeding.

As it turned out, this really did help me because about four months after doing this, I came upon a terrible accident while driving somewhere, and I felt no anxiety like I use to feel. I did take a moment to pray for those involved as well as the courageous first responders for providing aid and comfort to all involved.

Little did I know that this particular year's revelations only just began, the year that marked the tenth year since Sue died. My teaching assignments at the university began to slow down and would eventually stop by the end of the year. This would end my passion for teaching that I've always had and enjoyed doing for about twenty-six years. Knowing this was about to unfold, I began to seek other employment. I was leaving another comfort zone taking a risk.

I was hired into the social service field, a place I have never worked before. Learning a new job was where I placed my focus and energy. The position I held was at a county agency level, and I was an older employee compared to my coworkers, but that didn't bother me, nor did it bother them. I was warmly welcomed with kindness, and I was looked upon for my opinions and life experiences. I enjoyed working with dedicated and experienced coworkers who took their positions seriously and responsibly. They kept me interested in learning as much as I could and were kind enough to participate in my learning curve as I developed my skill set to provide service to clients.

This new beginning for me after a storied career in higher education, a small business owner, and a retail loss-prevention professional was just what I needed at the time. I met friendly people who would become longtime friends while learning the position I held in two different agencies. Helping people helped me. From children to parents, families to individuals, most needed a helping hand, guidance, resources, and a friendly smile to help them through an ordeal that is interfering with their daily life. I reflected that I was meant to do this at this time, just like I was meant to create the grief support group eight years ago for the need to help others. My mother died later in the year, almost three years to the day of my return from New England and ten years after my wife.

Four separate changes came within a twelve-month period, each one providing me with something different to deal with and continue on from where I once was. This is where it is necessary to look at change with a different perspective. Is this hurting me or helping me? Out of the four changes, one was very good getting over my fear and PTSD. Losing the opportunity to teach was dreadful but was replaced with a new career opportunity in social services. The loss of yet another family member, and especially your mom, takes its own toll no matter when that happens. Of course, the loss of my mom brought back the tragic loss of my wife and the loss of my father, whom I never really had a chance to grieve since his death was only two months before my wife.

When looking at this particular year, these changes were happening within a change—change 2—so this made things more complicated with dealing with all of this. I finally became free of anxiety associated with accident scenes, *a great thing*. My passion for teaching coming to a close, *an unfortunate thing*. Starting in a new field of endeavor, *a happy thing*; the death of my mother, *a sad thing*—there's a lot going on here.

I felt like I needed the following year to try to recover from this year. The twelfth year since Sue was killed was beginning, and the one constant was my dog Hal, who has kept me on track and somewhat sane as I continued on without her. I was so grateful for his presence and unconditional love and companionship.

I continued to struggle with my destiny still searching for my purpose even at this stage of my life. I solicited the counsel of a therapist with these issues and did receive some advice that guided me. I was reminded that it is me who can make the change. It's my choice. I have to be willing to take the risk to seek out another path to further my satisfaction in the life I now have. I also spent much time thinking about relationships I have with others. By others I mean family, close friends, and people I interacted with in general. I wish I felt closer to those in my life, and I blame myself for feeling isolated and not involved. It is I, for sure, a problem I can't seem to solve.

I believe that my relationships with everyone in my life were much stronger when my wife was alive. Her absence in my life placed me at a disadvantage with all of them. She was invested in me as a friend, loving partner, and husband and *always* had my best interests in mind. To this day, she is one in a million to me, and I love and miss her dearly.

As the fall season approached, something unexpectedly happened, and it involved Hal. Hal was about two weeks away from celebrating his fifteenth birthday when he had a seizure one evening right in front of me in our living room. In all the years of owning dogs, I never witnessed this before. It was heartbreaking, and I felt so helpless because there really isn't anything that can be done, except make them comfortable till it passes.

Calls were placed to the vet followed by visits to the vet over the course of the final ten weeks of the year. Medications were prescribed as Hal became weaker while additional seizures were happening to him. Hal's health was on a steady decline and just not himself with difficulty walking and even standing on his own. By the end of December, Hal crossed the rainbow bridge. Even with his advanced years for a medium-sized dog and some minor health issues in the last few years, I did not want to believe that he was no longer by my side.

The loss of Hal put me in a downward spiral of despair. Being without him would be a challenge for me and my efforts to continue to move forward. Hal was my rock and a representation of his master, my wife, Sue. His death made my mindset go back to the day that Sue died, and that was a place I was able to successfully keep on a shelf somewhere in an obscure part of my mind until now.

> Oh Lord, today I speak to you with great sadness in my heart. I've lost my beloved dog Hal. Lord, my heart aches, but I'm thankful for you. You brought me and Hal together, and throughout Hal's life, you granted him peace, happiness, and joy. Lord, I cannot thank you enough for the gifts you gave Hal. Now that my best friend has crossed the rainbow bridge, I ask that you watch over him with your loving heart. Thank you, Lord. Amen. (Pray.com)

Review of life change 2

I was in a position of renewal, rebirth, and growth while experiencing a feeling of relaxation and peace for the first time since her death, and I believe none of that would have been possible without the practice of forgiveness as being a major turning point in my approach and attitude toward life in general. I was now at a point of strength and at ease to deal with multiple changes this time around but confident to do so with the trust I've built on and the reliance of my dog for the many years he shared with me.

Reflections

Snow falls, memories resurface

Freshly fallen snow, white and silent as it accumulates outside my window. She made me look at snow in a whole new different way. We were in college, and it snowed. She decided to walk away from the shoveled path into the adventure of the drifts of snow that was around campus. I followed only to have the time of my life. We jumped through the snow, chased each other in the snow, made snow angels, threw snowballs at each other, made a snowman, and wrestled in the snow. When it was all said and done, I carried her in the snow. It's what she wanted all along. We laughed. We then headed indoors for warmth and some hot chocolate.

Those were the days. We fell in love, got engaged, and then married, and our times in the snow continued. We went sledding, continued to build snowmen, and the occasional snow ball battle was not out of the question. We loved to take walks in the snow while it was snowing to try to catch the snowflakes on our tongues and on a moonlit night, even better, so silent and illuminated. A stroll in the snow during Christmas was extra special with all of the holiday lights aglow.

Watching the snow now brings back these wonderful memories. I treasure these memories. And as it snows, whenever it snows, I reflect on past times of our beginnings as well as our entire life together.

Snow and winter make me remember. Perhaps the fall brings back memories for you—walks among the fallen leaves around a lake—or maybe the summer and time spent on a beach or on a vacation together. We all have triggers that allow us to remember happier times and are grateful that we experienced them with the one we love.

It was a great life I had with her, one that ended way too soon. Without her and her time with me, my life would not be as rich as it is today.

Stumbling on the past brings warm memories to the present

They were just there, right there, in front of me. I have seen them there many times over the years and never really thought about them or paused like I was doing right now. But now I did. I paused and stared at them. I am not really sure what I was thinking, but I stopped what I was doing to take in their sight and just froze in my tracks. I picked them all up, still in their original boxes from the times they were purchased.

That's how I am. I always seem to want to and actually do save original boxes of things, not big things but things that I feel are important to save because they are special, and these are special. At least that is what I am thinking right now as I hold them in my hands, but I guess they have always been special throughout the many years we had them. We cherished them, loved them, and respected them. We honored what they represented and knew what was behind their meaning and existence.

I stumbled upon them while I was looking in a drawer for something else, and I knew they were there but never really thought about them until now, at this moment. There were three small boxes. I opened all of them one at a time to look at the treasure before me, a treasure that was once worn by both of us.

The first box contained the engagement ring that I worked two summer jobs to pay for back in the '70s. The second box had her wedding band in that was custom-made with three diamonds that would match up to how the engagement ring was designed. This box also contained an eternity ring with five diamonds. I bought this for her on our twentieth anniversary. The third box was my wedding band. All of the pieces are in gold, and all appeared lifeless in their respective containers. Picking them up and really looking at them brought back such wonderful memories of a life that we were blessed to share with one another.

Details around how I proposed as well as our wedding day and the adventure of life that we were on together all came back to me. It was a warm and comfortable feeling and memories of a wonderful woman, wife, and mother.

Then I had the strangest desire to have them cleaned. It was something that had to be done and right now. Something that I would have considered silly years ago was now an objective. I took the rings into a local jeweler and had them cleaned. When I picked them up, they possessed a sparkle that I have never seen before even though they were cleaned countless other times. I am not sure why they appeared that way to me, but they did. I had to do this—get them cleaned. I had to go down that pathway of the past and bring that up again for me, and I am glad that I did. I felt at ease. I felt peace.

These rings are an important part of me—of us—still. I am not sure if they are something I will ever part with, at least not for now. But life continues to move forward, as do I.

Maybe there will be another time in the future when I will be looking for something and I come across them again, and then I guess we will see how I react to that. One never knows why we react and do things and feel things the way we do. We just do, and we have to accept and not question why.

Do what feels right on your journey, on your time line and no one else's. This is your journey. This is your new life without them. Take hold of life with both hands and know that you are not alone and that you can do this. You are a survivor, and nothing can stop you.

Maybe my wife wanted me to savor the moment of the redis-covery of the rings we both loved to wear. Who knows? It made my day, and I am glad for it. Sometimes, we never know what may be around the corner for us to encounter on this journey of ours. We must maintain faith and hope for a brighter tomorrow.

Silent pain

We walk among you, unknown and not noticed, hiding behind the mask that we wear more often than not to the rest of the world. We are people whom you are in contact with occasionally or perhaps daily within your circle of life. You may know our name and a little bit about us, but you really don't know us or what kind of pain we carry within our hearts.

Our pain is silent to you and only loud to ourselves. We are your neighbors, coworkers, or even the person you see walking past your house every now and then. We are the cashier at the convenience store or the delivery driver or perhaps your mailman. We can be the clerk at the front desk of the hotel you stayed at or the maid who cleaned your room. We can be your doctor or dentist, perhaps the last flight attendant you were in contact with.

Silent pain lives in silent homes, maybe a home with a pet or two. In our neighborhood, we wave or nod to you when we see you, and you return the gesture. Both of us are afraid about starting that conversation between us, and both of us wonder about the other. Early mornings and late nights, we find solace in the sound of the television or radio.

We lost a loved one, and although it was very painful in the beginning, things have improved for us to better handle things after some time. But the pain is still there, and at times, it comes to the surface very easily for us. We feel marked, and we keep silent because we don't want to hear the response you are going to give us when you first hear, nor do we want your sympathy. We actually feel bad when you feel bad for us, so we are silent.

Communicating among us happens in support groups if we have the courage to attend one. It is the one place we feel better about ourselves. We feel safe and understood—no judgments—and we can reveal our pain and shed the silence we keep among others who don't understand with those who do.

> The very familiarity of one's intimacy with grief heightens its poignancy for others. (Mayor, *The Catch*)

We become sensitive to people who probe us with questions and don't have the decency to let us be and allow us to grieve in our own way and at our own pace. If we don't have the courage for a group experience, talking with someone who understands can help ease the pain such as another person who also lost a loved one or a professional therapist or counselor. Another big step to take, but it does help you along your way after some time.

You begin to self-evaluate and realize that all of life is not lost. When tragedy strikes us, we see things differently from that point on. Any tragedy puts us in a different place. Our perspective and attitude changes, goals get reassigned, and priorities change. There is so much more out there that you can contribute to and to help others while helping yourself. Life is for the living, and you must learn to live again and free yourself from the silent pain that has been keeping you hidden from other people.

The still of the house

I miss the human side of how the morning comes and the day begins. The house is so still without her. No more touch on the shoulder or voice saying, "I love you," "Good morning," or "How did you sleep?" There is no more two-way conversation that fills the house. I miss that. I still speak to her at times, but the silence of the house is evident.

Through the shades and the curtains, nature provides the bright sun or raindrops on the window to announce the day and awaken me. Usually, the first sound heard in the morning is the birds singing outside my window, or sometimes it is the lone mourning dove on the window ledge with his early greeting.

I am dwarfed by a queen-size bed that at one time was too small on some nights for both of us. How I long to experience being crowded one more time.

The hearty bark of Hal, my dog, greets me as my feet hit the floor of my bedroom, which is above where he sleeps in the family room. I am so thankful for Hal and all that he has meant to me as the only other boarder in the house.

The only voices I hear are those from the electronic medium of our world: TV, radio, and those that are from songs we enjoyed together or those that I now enjoy alone that make me think of her.

The only footsteps heard are my own. The only lights that are on are for me. The dishwasher runs less, trash is hardly anything, and the washing machine whirls fewer times these days.

The kitchen is still. Nothing is stirring, not even a wooden spoon in a mixing bowl, for her talents in cooking and baking are no more, and dust settles on pots and pans that were once brimming with delicious recipes and baked goods.

I miss the scents of home-cooked meals, the smell of her hair, and the perfume of her choice. I miss the sounds of her presence: the running of the sewing or embroidery machine, the whistling tea kettle, her calling the dog, her voice on the phone, her playful laugh. The lack of it all contributes to the stillness I experience.

Even though I experience *the stillness of the house*, I am able to appreciate the memories that made it at one time full of life. I will always have love within my heart and soul for my wife. When I fell in love with her, it was forever.

Letters to heaven

I've been writing letters to heaven for a long time. My basic method is through journaling, plain and simple. But it doesn't have to be actual writing or writing in a journal. It could be through thoughts, wishes, hopes, even prayer. Whatever method, it's communication from you to whomever you are addressing your feelings to.

Communication through music and/or poetry can't be forgotten either. Many have written songs and expressed feelings through poems about the experiences they had with their loved ones or the experiences they have had since their parting. It's all good, healthy, and helpful.

This means provides an opportunity to say something you want to share about now or perhaps to say something you never got to say. I like to share events that are happening in my life at the moment, knowing that the one I lost is also experiencing it but in a different way, events that they are not a part of physically like they once were. I also use this time to ask questions about future decisions or seek guidance and acceptance, even direction or help with a problem. Feedback will not be vocalized, but I know I have received answers and direction in other ways. You have to believe, and you must be open to it.

There are times when my writing has turned into a diary of sorts, but that is okay because you are sharing thoughts and expressing feelings about your day without them, and it allows you to vent about life in writing. It provides a needed outlet for you where you are not judged and only you know what you have written since you control the privacy of your letters to heaven.

Writings can be all over the map with regard to context and emotion. Sometimes they are sad while other times they are happy and carefree. No matter how you feel, it should be reduced to writing and expression in communication of your thoughts and feelings. There is no pressure, no deadline, no rules when you pen a letter to heaven. It's you, and you're deciding what to write, when to write, and whom to write to.

And it is up to you to decide to keep what you wrote or discard it, share it or keep it to yourself, look back to what you wrote before or never return to what you once wrote. You have total control. Control is definitely something that helps you to realize that there are things that you are capable of controlling. Knowing that you have control over something helps you feel better about life since most times you are not in control of your own destiny or the destiny of others you love. So put pen to paper or type on a computer. Create a poem or write a song. It really does make you feel better. I've been journaling for twelve-plus years and have filled dozens of journals with my thoughts and feelings. Letters to heaven are always welcome.

Missing my better half

We all know the words, *Where's your better half?* as people refer to your partner, husband, or wife when they would see you without them on occasion or at events. The question meant a lot more than *Where is your partner?*

Deep down, it reflected something that none of us realized, the *better half* played an important role in our lives as a couple, and far too often, we took it for granted. I miss my better half. I believe my better half really was what the label implied.

She was the glue that kept things together in our lives. She was the planner, the organizer, the encourager, and the inspiration behind my successes. She made me feel comfortable about my life and living it to the fullest with her. She allowed me to grow and become things I never thought I'd be. She made me feel needed and wanted and never alone as I do now at times.

Those of us who have survived the death of our spouse knows that distinct feeling of aloneness that at times comes out of nowhere and overcomes us with great sadness. It is at those times when we know our better half is no longer with us to pick us up again. We miss them.

All of us at one time or many times have wished that the day it happened can be relived, and there would be something that we could do or something that could be done to prevent that tragedy from happening to them and to us. We wish that it was all a dream, and we would soon wake up from a very long nightmare, and life as we knew it would return.

It is not going to happen. We have to acknowledge this and understand that we probably can try to replace some of those feelings we experienced from our better half's involvement with another partner or a close friend or family member. We can also try to focus on ways that we can become a better person by ourselves through involvement with other activities that are rewarding to us and make us feel better.

Although my better half is no longer with me, she will always be within my heart and close to my soul, providing a comfort level that only she knew how to do.

Memories

Even without triggers, we like to recall past events and make them be present with us. We like to look at pictures, handle an item or two, remember a scent, a look, a smile, the way a voice sounded. It can even be how the wind blows on certain days that make us remember or the warmth of a sunset or sunrise that brings on a memory.

Being with nature can have many effects on us too: sounds of wind blowing through a forest or a brook flowing against rocks, sounds of the ocean or birds singing. Everyday noises that are usually distractions can also be a gateway into a world full of past memorable moments.

Just the past weekend, I came across two obscure happenings: old songs and T-shirts. I came across a cassette of old songs that we shared a love for, and I played it, and it happened to me. The memories came flowing back: beautiful, loving memories of times past. So vivid they were, I could actually envision us (my wife and I) together. It was wonderful.

I also was going through dresser drawers and came across T-shirts, T-shirts that were significant of a time and a place, where we were or what we were attending, a souvenir of a past event that brought back those memories like it was yesterday. Some of these were mine, and others were hers that I had to keep and still love having. I wear them to this day, and it makes me smile when I see them and wear them, knowing what they represent for both of us and especially why they mean more to me than ever before.

It doesn't matter how you come across memories. It matters that you continue to have them and use them to your advantage of remembering a happy time when you were together. Be thankful for building those memories with your loved one and still celebrating them to this day.

Nothing stays the same

Change is something that we love and hate. Many of us need change and need it often. We're not satisfied with the way things are for too long and must make a change to something else, something different, something newer, something easier. That's our choice. Some of us like the way things are and hope change doesn't happen. We want it to be the same and don't invite change. We're satisfied and happy with what we are, what we have, who we're with, and where we live. That's our choice.

There are those of us who are a little of both. We like the way things are but are not afraid or reluctant to a change here and there. Our thoughts are that change is good sometimes. When something remains the same, life becomes stale, stagnant, boring. Some of us require change more often and dislike when things stay the same too long. Desiring change often makes life interesting, exciting, adventurous and challenges our souls to keep up with ourselves, our drive.

When examining our life and taking the time to reflect on where we have been and where we are now, it will become clear that nothing stays the same. In spite of ourselves and our willingness to be the master of our destiny, it doesn't matter. Change is inevitable. Change will happen. Change is part of life. It's difficult for us to accept something that we have no control over, like the changes in our lives that happen suddenly and unexpectedly. This kind of change is not our choice.

My wife, Sue, died suddenly and unexpectedly, and believe me, everything changed. Life as I once knew it stopped, and it took years for a restart. The new beginning for me was just that—all new. I never had to think about life without her since I met her in college some thirty years ago. Change was happening, and it was noticeable and at times uncontrollable. None of us in a loving and healthy relationship think it's ever going to end even though we all know that death is the final act of life.

Nothing stays the same for any of us during what we call normal times because life happens, and choices are made. When tragedy strikes, it's all hands on deck. Death changes everything. Each baby step you take puts you in another place and a different state of mind, less of who you once were and more of somebody you don't even know yet. What you do, where you work, how you live, who you talk to, what you believe, how you feel, why you hurt, how you express yourself can all change.

Most times, these changes are happening so fast and being driven by uncertainty, emotion, fear of the unknown, and the desire to feel better than you do right at that moment. You're in shock, and you will be for some time. It's tough to be grounded at all. I remember saying, *I don't know what to do*, to myself and at times repeatedly out loud to those around me. And I didn't. I was clueless.

There are things that have to be dealt with in a timely manner, and they come first, and you are reminded of them by those who require you to do them. That is priority. Everything else is secondary and later, much later. As time passes and you begin to feel some sense of togetherness, you slowly begin to function in a basic fundamental way. This is where the changes come in, and you will hopefully be able to think about them with some sense of clarity.

Change will project you into a future of unknown, a future of who you will now be. You are no longer the person you once were when you had your spouse with you. Some of us will wait at least a year or more before making any real big changes while others are ready way before then. It is really up to the individual, and most times, it is encouraged, when in doubt, to seek advice from a trusted friend, family member, or professional.

I don't know of anyone who has been through losing a spouse who hasn't changed the way they look at life. Many changed their lives through relocations, career changes, retirement, volunteering, faith, hope, prayer, journaling, helping others, peace, exploration, and attitude. Whatever changed for you, beware. Another change may be coming because nothing stays the same.

From the way we were to the who I am

Webster's Dictionary defines transition as "a passing from one condition, place, etc. to another." Most transitions eventually can be defined as a transformation, a change of the form or condition of. That is kind of what happens when a transition from *we* to *I* occurs.

I am one of many who experienced a transition in their life when my wife died suddenly and unexpectedly many years ago. The transformation was sudden and unexpected as well, and I certainly wasn't looking forward to what was about to become a reality. It was frightening. It was uncertain. It was a transformation I wasn't ready for. But who could be?

In those early days of the tragedy, I wasn't sure how I would survive day-to-day, let alone months or years later. So many thoughts and emotions and feelings of helplessness and hopelessness occupied most of my time, and I could not control it or stop it from happening to me. I was transformed into a world I knew nothing about, a world without the love of my life who had been there for me for some thirty years.

I began to journal my thoughts. I sought out and attended a bereavement support group. I went to a therapist for counseling. I applied forgiveness. And all of that helped me understand where I was and provided me with searching my own soul to determine where I needed to be and how I needed to get there.

I was blessed with resources that most people don't have to take huge risks and big moves to help my journey of rediscovery. Through leaps and bounds that brought me through some low valleys, I survived when it was all said and done. I learned from my adventure and grew as an individual and became someone whom I would have never recognized before the journey began.

I can only speak for myself but offer to you that in order to move forward with one's life after a tragedy, you have to be willing to take chances, make choices, and forgive. And even if they don't work to your satisfaction, it may have taken you to a place that will help you later in life. You may not know that at the time, but it will become apparent in the future.

It is amazing what the human spirit, a good attitude, and a positive outlook can do for you. It may feel like the world came crashing down upon you, and there are cloudy skies with a storm brewing, but you have to go through all of that in order to see the sun again and if you are lucky, a rainbow too.

You can't stay in a place of sorrow. You must make the transition from *the way we were* to the *who I am* and accept the new transformation of the new you, a person who wants to live, laugh, and love again and become the best that you can be for yourself and the friends and family around you.

We all have a story

Losing a loved one can make us feel all alone. We feel like it has happened to us and only us and that no one else out there understands what we are going through. Some of our friends stop calling, and at times, it seems they are trying to avoid us when we really need them to be there for us. Not everyone handles the grief of another in the way we would like them to, and it is not their fault. Our society has trouble understanding and acknowledging grief and all that it encompasses.

Your personal story of tragedy is yours alone, but one must realize that *we all have a story*. Knowing that there are others who have stories of the loss of a loved one allows us to realize that we are not alone. Although everyone's story is different in many ways, the true similarities come forward when they are being shared among the attendees of a bereavement support group.

People with similar losses will have similar feelings and will be able to identify with each other with their feelings. A bond amongst them will be created, and it is at that moment that you realize in a very small way that you have something in common within the grief process that is happening among you.

Seeing a therapist, counselor, or attending a support group is also very helpful during the bereavement process. Telling one's story is what it's all about. During appointments with trained professionals, what you express allows the listener to comment and pose questions to you that allow you to search your own being and reflect on what is happening within you at the time. After some time, you begin to reflect on your own and are able to turn your negative feelings into positive actions of moving forward.

Telling our story helps us. Each time it is told, whether in detail or a short summary, it allows us to express and hear our own words in our voice tell how it is. This provides acknowledgment and comfort to us. This empowers us. This telling of our story becomes easier with time, and we recognize how helpful it is over time.

It may be difficult to share with others, especially the others who are strangers to you in a group setting. Trust me. The strangers who are gathered hurting from a loss like you will become friends who come together to share thoughts and feelings. Together, you will be there for each other, and together, you can help each other heal.

Life Change 3

Hal's death changed everything. I realized how important Hal was to my own survival after Sue died, and I was leaving a comfort zone I got used to for the last twelve years. I was now on my own, and I needed help. I went back to see a therapist and also attended a pet-loss support group for the help I needed to get by.

I felt defeated. I was at a very low point and did not want to drag anyone else down with me. I knew in my heart I needed space to be alone with my grieving the loss of Hal and therefore reduced as many distractions around me as possible. That full year after the death of Hal placed me in isolation, or I should say I placed myself there. I moved slowly along the way as I recovered from the loss and adjusted to a new life without his presence. The year was the necessary grieving and needing recovery, and I just wasn't in a good place since his death late December of 2017.

I am aware of those who judged my reaction to losing a pet and couldn't understand how one could be that affected by it, but as I have written many times before, Hal was more than a pet to me. He was a valued member of our family. Those of you with pets know how much they become family members and are such a part of your daily life in everything you do. I could not have survived the horrific loss of my wife without his presence and devotion to my needs. I was blessed that Hal was with me as many years as he was to guide and comfort me. His death made me realize how much I depended on him to get me through life without Sue.

After a full year of learning to live without Hal, with grief support at its highest level for me since those first few years when my wife died, I spent the following year trying to decide if I should pursue another dog. Although I know firsthand all the benefits that I have gained from dog ownership in the past, I decided against this. I'm just not equipped to go through another heartache from the loss of a pet again. But at the same time, I was thinking of another change.

After Sue died, continuing on in the job I had was more difficult for me, and I debated whether to stay until finally deciding to walk away and try something different with my life. The same thing was happening with Hal's death. Is it time to move on from the job I currently have to something else? And the something else I was thinking of was retirement.

Her premature death made me think about how short life is to all of us. I decided to walk away from the work world, collect social security that I paid into over the years, and enjoy what life has to offer me. My wife, Sue, never had that opportunity, nor do many others who die too young. In my opinion, none of us are guaranteed good health in our later years. The future is nothing but uncertainty. Life is fragile and short. If you can retire early, do it.

December 2019 arrived, and I gave a four-week notice to my employer that I was retiring at the end of the month. A new kind of life will begin for me, being unemployed by choice and hoping to explore and do other things with my time and talents. Another risk to be taken at a time that I need to make another change. Perhaps a sign to acknowledge, accept, and adapt to a new part of my life. Without realizing it at the time, my last day on the job was the day Hal died exactly two years ago.

Within the first quarter of the new year and the first year being retired, the world as we knew it changed with experiencing a pandemic of global proportions. Stay-at-home orders became the norm. Wearing a face mask was part of our dress code. Small businesses went out of business. Schools and some workplaces went virtual. Delivery services were created. Grocery and retail shelves went empty. Experiencing this life-altering situation *alone* was difficult. There was no one in the same household to talk with, share, worry, or pray together.

Everyone proceeded with caution and had to adapt their lives to restrictions of work, school, and play. I decided to look into putting together a collection of reflections that I have been writing over the years for other publications and my own newsletter. Putting that together provided a cathartic experience for me in my own review of my emotions and thoughts. I also decided to include actual entries from my personal journals. Never thinking this had the chance for publication, I was encouraged by a literary agent who represented a publisher to submit my manuscript. I did, and it was accepted for publication. *Miss Your Forever* was published in December of 2020.

As the world continued to hobble along addressing the pandemic, my second full year of retirement continued to involve writing a memoir based on my personal grief time line. This involved a deeper look into my actual journey that included a thirteen-year time frame. I also included entries from my personal journals. My manuscript was accepted by the same publisher, and *In a Heartbeat* was published in March of 2022.

Sharing your story can be helpful and healthy if you are willing to take that chance and be somewhat vulnerable. Whether expressing yourself privately to a nonjudgmental friend or therapist or even making entries in a private journal that only you see, it is all good and positive steps in the right direction. Grief support groups can provide a safe place to be, to listen, and to share your story. Telling your story won't bring your loved one back. Telling your story won't take your pain away. But telling your story at the right time among broken souls like yourself is what saves your life again and again. I did all of the above and then took a leap of faith and shared my story through speaking and writing for all to hear and read.

Writing became a focus of mine during retirement in addition to volunteer activity, roasting coffee, meeting up with old friends, and enjoying my time as I chose without any schedule, deadline, or place I had to be. I also continued facilitating the support group sudSSpirit, which I created and now had more time to devote to and help others individually who were struggling with their grief journey. In 2023, the support group achieved the fifteen-year mark of helping hundreds of people heal as they processed their grief over the years.

Retirement wasn't supposed to be me alone, but it is, and there isn't anything I can do to change that. Sue's sudden death placed me in this position. I cherish the beautiful memories that I have and recognize how blessed and grateful I am for the time I did spend with Sue and how her love for me made me the man I am today.

Since I retired, I have been visiting two seniors occasionally who have lost their spouses, two souls from two different localities who don't know of each other but share a common heartache. I have become the common denominator to talk with them, share my thoughts, and help guide and direct them through their individual pain of grief. I, being twenty years their junior and having gone through my own loss of a spouse, still struggle with their display of emotions as I continue to cope with my own.

Nothing usually stays the same after a death: happenings that we are comfortable with, situations that we love to be in, family events and holiday traditions, places we like going, feelings we experience, and smiles we make. I have also realized how we experience the following has changed: laughter, sorrow, attitude, ambition. outlook, regrets, choices, risks, anxiety, fear, depression, relationships, and family dynamics. Death changes us, and we will never be the same as we once were.

There are still difficult moments that happen for me. It is those times that sadness overwhelms me, and I need to be alone and cry and pray for a better day to come. And like a saving grace, I connect with a friend. We have a nice, long talk connecting with warm memories of good times during a past when the world was a kinder place.

What can I say about my new life without her? While you are trying to get it together, survive, exist, be somewhat normal to others and adjusting to yourself now that things are so different, life marches on. You have done things that you never desired, wanted, or intended before because it wasn't just you who was involved. It was you plus your soulmate, your spouse, your partner.

It continues to be a paradox for me. Whenever I decide on a change or make a choice, think about a decision or take a risk—and there is a good outcome—there is *no one* to whom I can share the joy. The *no one* used to be my wife, Sue. The change, choice, decision, or risk is done out of necessity to live a life without her presence, and it's her very presence that is lacking in the celebration of the positive event that happened. I wouldn't be doing any of this if she never died. It was what had to be done in order for me to make a move forward. I will never forget our time together, and I'll never stop loving her.

It is often said that you never really know a person. When you look at family members, as close as you can be, there are just some issues and topics that don't come up or are never asked, and that goes for couples too. We knew each other for thirty years, but I bet there was still so much we didn't know about each other. There were probably experiences each of us has had or lessons we learned that we haven't shared and now never will. I guess I look back at all of this now in hindsight and wish I was given a second chance to talk more with her. Conversation is what I have missed the most over the years, along with the sound of her voice, her laugh, and her smile.

I believe it is so easy to have an unknown, unexplored, unseen silence between people and not even know it. It is never too late to change the relationship we have with someone important in our life: a parent, spouse, partner, child, or friend. It takes courage and a willingness to be honest and drop your guard and let go of the long-standing assumptions or beliefs you may be holding on to between each other. We all want to experience a transformative moment where we suddenly see our future and the person we are meant to be. We all should strive to be our authentic self and seize the moment. Let's be real with each other.

My daily walk around my neighborhood is a great opportunity to reflect, meditate, and think random thoughts. Sitting on my deck has its own advantages with soaking up the warm rays of the sun while listening to a particular bird singing in the distance. After sunset, admiring the starlit sky and the brightness of the moon as the crickets and lightning bugs entertain my senses.

You aren't necessarily lonely when you are alone. Being alone, at times, is the greatest feeling in the world for me. Reading a book with soft music in the background. Writing when I have something significant to say. Thinking with a pad of paper and pen in front of me for notes, thoughts, and doodling. Walking on a trail within nature's beauty. Sitting on a bench while just being in the moment, listening to the sounds around you. Enjoying a favorite beverage while sitting in your favorite chair. Going through a box of memories and being grateful.

I'm feeling a new reality among my days, more enriched with life around me. My perspective of life has taken on a new meaning and is coming together, providing me with a sense of freedom, renewal, and faith.

Review of life change 3

The death of my dog Hal began this all-important life change. Mourning Hal for an entire year was the beginning of a transition for me, once again making choices and taking risks. I decided to retire and enjoy my time without the confines and restrictions of the work world.

Three months into that time, the world closed down for an unprecedented pandemic, not only placing everyone's life at risk but also into different directions. I continued with my writing and facilitating my grief support group and spent time reflecting on my past life experiences while philosophizing on the future.

Will there be more life changes?

Of course. If I learned anything on this journey of grief and life, it is that nothing stays the same. Life changes can be both negative and positive. When all is said and done, it all evens out.

Reflections

Opening a box of memories

> For whatever reason, I opened one of two memory boxes repacked by both of us in 1997. I cried, remembered, and smiled. It's nice to know that they are there for whenever I need them to be.
> (an entry from my journal, July 2018)

I remember the repacking of the memory boxes like it was yesterday. My wife and I had moved into this house about four years prior and never really had time to go through all that we brought with us from the former house. We were thinking of a yard sale and decided to rummage through things to see what we didn't want or need anymore. We came across a variety of saved items as well as dozens of handwritten letters from our days of dating in college and engagement, and they were in multiple boxes, so as we discovered them, we gathered them to place all together in two boxes and marked them memories and taped them shut.

Looking back, when we were married and combining possessions, we both realized that we saved things that the other gave us, such as cards, small souvenirs, movie stubs, play programs. It didn't surprise me that Sue saved all the letters I wrote to her. What surprised Sue (and myself) was that I saved all of her letters to me. I personally never looked at any of the saved items or letters over the years. I can't say the same for Sue. At the time of the repacking in two labeled boxes in 1997 and taped closed, these boxes were never opened by either of us until I opened one of them in 2018.

As reflected in my journal entry above, I thought I may be ready to strut down memory lane at that point of my grief journey. I wasn't. I acknowledged their presence and thought another time I'll be ready. I retaped the box and forgot about it.

Fast-forward four years to 2022 and on a random weekend, I was ready to open the box of memories. As what happened four years ago, I cried just looking at the contents before me. Then I smiled as I began to touch and sort through items as I remembered milestones of a relationship that was just beginning in the '70s. I was ready this time, but I knew I had to pace myself, knowing there will be moments when I will say enough for now. I'll stop and come back later.

The past memories of our beginning just flowed through me. It was like opening a time capsule of our young love for each other. Seeing my "late teens, early twenties" handwriting on letters and cards felt strange but reminiscent. Besides what all of the contents of these memory boxes represent of a college couple in love, I treasure the handwriting of my dear Sue as well as the content of the letters that we had so earnestly written and mailed to one another. Photographs and items saved from our humble honeymoon many years ago represent two in love with not much money but a future rich in the desire to be together for eternity.

When you reflect like this and there are memories in your hands touched by your hands and those of your partner long ago, it almost transcends time, and for a brief moment, you are there, back there with the feeling of invincibility, and nothing will stand in your way of achieving great things with each other having the other's back. What a feeling that was at the time.

This was not something that can be done at any time after the loss of your loved one. You must be ready for it with a box of tissues and be aware of the vulnerability it will put you through. And if it takes sixteen years like it did for me or longer, that's okay. Some of us may never have the courage to go back and look, touch, smell, read, remember, and that's okay too. We are all different in how we process our grief and how we decide to react to it. Wishing you all peace and comfort in however you deal with your memories.

Taking a bike ride with a memory or two

On a beautiful Sunday afternoon when the weather was too nice to not be outdoors, I decided on a bike ride on a trail near my home. Many others had the same idea as I pulled into the crowded trailhead parking lot. Couples, families, and some pets, too, came along to enjoy the sunshine. A mix of walkers and joggers were also present.

Bike rides are different for me now: solo. My wife and I rode our bikes together on many bike trails around the current home we were occupying at the time. When our daughter came along and she was able, she accompanied us. For many years, this was a favorite pastime, sharing the outdoors with the ones you love, doing something healthy and fun.

As time passed and my daughter matured, she did not want to be part of the Mom-Dad bike ride, so it came down to the two of us, and that was okay. Years later with knee trouble, my wife dropped out and then took up kayaking. We would then drive to a lake that also had bike trails, and although we did separate healthy and fun things, we enjoyed the drive to and fro and then the conversation of how our experience was.

As I biked on this mostly shaded trail today, this is what I was remembering: our talks, laughs, betting who could get to the next marker first and seeing who could be less out of breath. Memories like it were just yesterday, happy and fun memories of times passed.

I smiled and said hello to so many people who were on the trail today, thinking of the times they were sharing with each other at that moment as a couple or with children whether walking or biking. I also thought of those who were by themselves like me, men and women alone taking a walk, jog, or bike ride. What's their story? Time alone from their spouse or family; single, divorced, widowed—maybe they were reflecting the same thing I was.

Riding my bike now has a new meaning for me, a good one. I have come so far on my journey and still enjoy riding a bike. It provides a feeling of freedom and allows me to think and remember all the good times I shared with my wife and daughter. I am comforted with being on a trail and out in nature, feeling content and satisfied. I am so happy for those moments and all the other moments I shared with them. It is so important to spend time with those you love right now. Time is something that, when taken away, can never be returned to you. Enjoy your time and create moments with your loved ones.

Life is defined in moments. I am glad that there were these past moments in my life so that I can have fond memories now.

The change of the season

As the first day of spring came, I am reminded of all the *firsts* we experience in our lives. Our entire life is built upon firsts. From infancy, we celebrate firsts in our lives and the lives of our family and friends. First steps, first birthday, first tooth, first day of school, graduation, first car, first job, marriage, first child, first house, first grandchild, and it goes on and on.

We celebrate and share firsts with those whom we love. We build a life of firsts with those whom we love. As the firsts happen and we continue with our lives, it's taken for granted and becomes part of our lives that all of these kinds of things will happen with a companion, a partner, a wife or husband. That is the beauty of life itself that we are able to share events and happenings with those whom we love, and the sharing is what makes it all so special.

When we lose someone very close to us, the firsts of life as they continue without our loved one are looked upon differently. It becomes difficult to be part of a first-time event or situation alone. You may have friends and family with you during these firsts, but it is not the same without your partner. You feel it, and it makes you very sad. At times, this can become overwhelming to you that you put off these firsts because you just can't do it yet. That's okay. You will know when you are ready to tackle the challenge of dealing with something for the first time without your loved one.

Being ready will not mean that it will be easy. The first time you go to an appointment alone may even be difficult and something that you avoid for a while. The first time you go grocery shopping alone or to a movie alone may be difficult. The first time you come home to an empty house will have its own impact on you. The first time you are out with others and there are more couples than those who are there alone will bother you.

The calendar year will play its role with you as well. All of those first holidays, birthdays, and anniversaries without your loved one will be struggle for you because you are used to sharing those moments with them. Sometimes, the second, third, and fourth years may be difficult too. The day of the week and the date of their passing may affect you.

These are struggles that we have in common, struggles that are unknown by those who aren't experiencing this. You will eventually be able to handle all of these, some easier than others, but you will handle them. There are some things I have yet to do, go through, let go of, become, visit, and talk about. But these things in my own time frame will be completed someday.

The change of the season provides us with a new outlook, especially springtime: new growth, new birth, new beginnings. It is up to us to either dwell on another season as it changes and stay trapped in negative thoughts and feelings or to embrace it, be positive, and make it the best that we can as we move forward one season at a time.

Her last two-year planner

How many of you use your phones or another electronic device to record your appointments, comings and goings, events, vacations, days off, etc.? Probably most of you. I'm still old-school and have to purchase a pocket-size calendar/planner annually to record important dates and events of my daily life throughout the year. And then at the end of the year, I would store it away and eventually discard it years later.

Recently, I was trying to remember a date when something happened years ago and went to my archive of personal calendars to try to find it. Not only was I able to find what I was looking for, but I discovered my wife's last two-year planner/calendar. I forgot I even kept it. I immediately froze in my thoughts and actions and held it with reverence.

Here was a historical review of events and daily happenings in her handwriting on calendar pages from the last year she was alive. I stopped what I was doing at the time and sat down to page through the final year of her life on earth. It actually started on the last month of the previous year. Most of it was her work schedule, but it also included the date we saw a Christmas play, a weekend trip we took to Chicago, and the Saturday we got our Christmas tree that year.

As I paged through the last year of her life, there were doctor's appointments, Hal's vet and grooming appointments as well as Hal's schedule for his therapy visits, notes on a winery tour weekend we spent in the finger lakes in New York, my teaching schedule, the last Broadway play we attended, her hair appointments, our yard sale we had on Memorial Day weekend, dates when our daughter was coming home, and vacation weeks that we were off together. Turning the page onto to the month of January, it was difficult not to focus on her birthday, a Friday, with a note that I was off for it and the following Monday, with her scheduled time for work, which she never arrived for due to the accident that killed her. Going into February, it was clearly marked a full week of our long-awaited and planned trip to Belgium and Amsterdam, which I would be canceling shortly after her death.

Tears flowed freely onto the pages of this open calendar while staring at her handwriting and remembering all of these events once noted by a very much alive and vibrant woman I loved very much. It seemed to me to be another lifetime ago, another realm of time where we once existed in love and harmony, a place that no longer exists and I can never experience again.

I looked at my personal calendar/planner and realized that whether it is written or entered digitally, this becomes our system of life organization for us to complete and reference.

What we fail to recognize is that someday, our record will become known and reviewed by someone else, and it may very well be a loved one who will cherish the mundane notes, remarks, and life's activities that were, at one time, of great importance to the writer. And seeing this will bring tears and joy to whoever is reading this, knowing that this person who was loved so deeply by us will forever be in our hearts. I miss and love you, Sue. Your spirit lives within me.

Life experiences

The experiences of life that we go through are as diverse as our individuality, some things we never experience or are limited to what we do experience depending on our paths of life that we chose or were chosen for us. Some of us experience many things for the same reasons.

But no matter where you fall into this spectrum of life, whatever you experience makes you the person you are. Add to that the people around you while you are experiencing it, and that changes it up a little. Add the location that it is happening in, as well as your age, and that increases the meaning behind it as well.

Life-changing situations can be either planned or unexpected. They can be hoped for, wished, dreamed about, think they will never happen, or pray that they never come to be. We cannot control them as we cannot control life and our destiny.

So we think of those milestone in one's life and reflect: birthdays, birthdays that have more meaning (sixteenth, eighteenth, twenty-first, thirtieth, fortieth, fiftieth), youth sports leagues, first job, clubs in high school, dating, honors, awards, high school graduation, college life, dean's list, honors, awards, falling in love, college graduation, first job out of college, career decisions, getting married, having children, moving/relocating, changing jobs, divorce/separation, losing jobs, death of a friend, death of loved ones (parents, spouse, children). These milestones, life experiences, happenings, life phases, or whatever you want to label them changes us in a small or large way.

However, this affects us, and it does make a difference in our lives, a difference that is never really noticed at the time it is happening, but it is there, and it is making us different than we were before. Any one of them can be a pivotal point in our life that enables us to change our outlook, attitude, and outcome for the present time and at times for the future.

As I reflect about one of my life-changing experiences, the one that changed everything, the sudden, unexpected death of my wife, I can see how my world as I knew it ceased to exist, and another one took its place. I did not have a choice. It came fast and out of the blue, and I was right in the middle of it before I knew what really happened.

Everything changed—my attitude, opinions, thoughts, feelings, ambitions, desires, needs, wants, challenges, goals, what I thought about life, friends, family, colleagues, work, money, success, happiness, love, heartache, sex, friendship, charities, strangers. What was once important was no longer, and what was never thought about was always on my mind.

The changes in me as an individual did not happen all at once, nor were they seen by others right away, but they were there, and they were making me become someone I never was before. This new person I became was good and bad for me. When you are experiencing many changes in your being, you begin to have much self-doubt and uncertainty about your life and your future.

Eventually, you lose friends who were close to you and your spouse, people at work treat you differently, and new people whom you meet are cautious about what to say and don't really know who you are. You are one, and you are alone. And one really is a lonely number, as the song implies. It becomes a balancing act. You're on a high wire, and there is no net below to save you. It's up to you to pursue and keep moving forward one baby step at a time with no regrets.

This is also a new beginning for you, one that you have to create and do something with your newfound feelings and attitude about life and your future. I started to appreciate the little things more. I began to take no one for granted. I realized who the most important people in my life were. I finally knew what mattered and what was important about living and life. I began to take chances and take risks.

Each day is a gift as well as a risk. I shared more of my feelings with people I liked and respected. I reached out to those I have not seen or heard from in a while. I searched for ways to contribute my talents and skills to causes and others in need. In a way, I kind of re invented myself. As much as I liked the old me and did not want to leave who I once was, I knew that person left with the death of my wife, and there was no going back.

It may take years for you to realize all that I just said here, or perhaps you already have experienced some of this. Whatever the situation, please know that you are not alone in this. There are countless others going through the same thing. Life threw us a curveball, and we are trying to hit one out of the park toward a brighter future.

As fall begins

It was a beautiful Saturday morning with a sky of blue and the temps in the midseventies. I decided a walk along a familiar trail was in order. Walking among what nature has to offer cleanses the mind and provides a necessary outlet for anxiety amid the busy world that is around us. Hearing the crunch of the gravel as your footsteps become a cadence of your steps along your way combined with the birds chirping, the creek meandering along the trail to the left side, and the remnants of an old canal to your right, providing a historical reference to this perfect-weather day.

I was not alone because others saw the opportunity to take advantage of this early fall weather to be outside, enjoying the sights and sounds of nature as it provides nourishment to our souls. Walkers, joggers, bikers, families, couples, and those of us who are venturing out on this day alone.

This trail I speak of is the Union Canal Trail in Berks County, and my choice today was the section between the Heritage Center and Rebers Bridge. Almost four miles round trip of beauty, stillness, and peace. I have walked or biked this trail countless times over the years, most of which with my wife, Sue, and at times with our daughter. Not much has changed over the years as I walk this trail. Some old trees have been replaced with new ones, but the path itself remained the same all this time.

There was not a sliver of a breeze as I walked to the turning point, and throughout that walk, I remembered my life with my wife and all the good times we shared together over the years. As I walked back on my return trip, I thought of how much I missed her and wished she was alongside me making this walk more enjoyable. That thought no sooner came to mind when a comfortable, cool breeze developed on the trail followed by both of my arms getting goosebumps and a feeling of a presence around me of love and joy. I rubbed my arms to counter the goosebumps and smiled, knowing she was near. I stopped for a moment and savored the time and looked to the sky and thanked her for being part of this experience. As I continued on my walk, the breeze subsided, not to recur again for the rest of the walk.

I am fortunate that even after these many years, I still feel connected to her. I am open to the possibility to receive signs from her, and I frequently do. Today was one of those times. You just have to believe and be patient, and it may happen to you.

Connecting with nature and the outdoors has always been a way for me to feel present in the moment. Because if you are not in the moment, you're probably thinking of the past or pondering the future. If so, you are not enjoying the *now*. Being present makes you enjoy life as it is right now and then with no worries of the future and no regrets from the past. It's a great time to just *be*. Your stress level will decrease along with your heart rate and blood pressure, and you will allow yourself to breathe easier and be calm about the life you are experiencing.

As my walk ended, I took advantage of the Canal Museum being open as well as the Gruber Wagon Works and learned a little about the history behind this area and what life was like back then for that period of time. The very trail I just walked was a tow path one time for mules to pull a canal boat along the way, transporting goods and coal to places beyond. This was actually the first time I was ever inside the museum or the wagon works. Sue and I never had that opportunity all the time we visited that part of the trail. I think she was with me that day. That made me smile.

The best that you can do

One of the most difficult issues I have been dealing with since my wife, Sue, died is my search for where I should be in life, not just where in terms of what I should be doing and for what purpose but also the where in terms of geographical location. A struggle that I have yet to conquer, but I keep trying.

One never knows the contentment and satisfaction one feels with their life until a life-changing moment occurs, like the death of your spouse or significant other, and then you have to rethink your future all over again. Your world turned upside down. The rug was pulled out from under you, a physical and mental challenge to your body and mindset: what do you do now?

At times, I think I am the only one with this problem or at least the only one who is this distraught over this effect it has on me and how much time I spend dwelling on it. Others I have spoken to are coming along fine, maintaining their daily schedules and lives and pretty much are where they have been but minus the one they loved so dear. I am happy for them. Others have made some changes. Perhaps they relocated to another home or apartment, moved to another town to be closer to family, or moved in with another person. I am happy for them also.

I have accepted my grief journey, and I have accepted what has happened to me, and I strive to help others with their journeys of grief, but I have not accepted where I should be or what I should be doing or where I should be doing it. People I speak to about this dilemma of mine say that I am searching for something that does not exist. Others say that my searching is what I am doing and is where I should be: meeting new people, helping others, relocating, trying new things, learning, exploring, writing, sharing. Be happy with the present, the now, they say. Don't overthink it.

I am not sure what the answer is, if there is an answer. I sometimes think that I am overthinking it, but I can't deny that I feel like something is missing in my life, something tangible as well as spiritual, and that is "this search" I speak about.

I have made so many changes and decisions. I have allowed myself to explore, create, meet head-on, switch, become vulnerable, take risks, cry, laugh, express, and pray. Some of the things I planned out methodically, while others were spur-of-the-moment ideas that I carried out to see what would happen. Whatever the case, no regrets. I did it, and doing it made me feel worthwhile and in control of my own destiny for that moment in time.

And then, I needed more. It seems I am never content with where I am and what I am doing. I look back at my life with my spouse, and I was very content with where I was, sharing a life with her. Am I looking for that missing piece that I lost when I lost her? And after this many years, should I finally realize that I will never be able to duplicate that?

So what's the answer? Is there an answer? Is this really a problem? It can be one man's search for a destiny he has yet to encounter. Will the search be endless? Perhaps the search should never end, for the search is part of the life I now lead.

Whatever the future holds for me, I know that change is inevitable, and nothing really stays the same. A common expression voiced by many is this: "It is what it is, but it will become what you make it."

So many lives within a lifetime

> You only Live once. In my previous Life. Such is
> Life. Life happens. Life is like a novel, it's filled
> with suspense. You have no idea what is going to
> happen until you turn the page.

The other day, I was with a few friends, and one of them made reference to the way something was handled where he had worked before, and he prefaced it with these words, "In my previous life, we did it this way." Everyone knew the reference point being of a past time, past employer, or past career. It made me think that we all have those moments in life that are like a totally different life than where we are right now. And those previous moments constitute many lives that we experienced.

> Life is what you make it. Life goes on. Life doesn't
> stop for anybody. Let me live my Life. Death is
> not the opposite of Life, but a part of it. Life is
> a gift.

So thinking of it that way, how many lives will we have in a lifetime? If I share my own list, I guess my first *life* was the life I had growing up with parents and a sibling, friends in the neighborhood to friends at school till high school graduation. My second *life* happened when I went to college, and for those four years with new friends and experiences, I grew as an adult, met the girl of my dreams, and fell in love. Life number 3 is when I got married to the girl I met in life number 2. My third *life* ended with her death, therefore starting a fourth *life*, a life without her.

> Life will break you. This Life's hard. Life is about
> not knowing. Life is pain. Enjoy your Life. Accept
> what Life offers you. It's your Life.

There are also sublives within lives that enhance our beings and character, like when or if we became a father or mother, aunt or uncle, grandparent. Changing jobs or relocating or starting a hobby can be a sublife within a life. My teaching experience was part of my third and fourth life, therefore being part of two lives. Opening a business was a sublife for me, as was entering a new career in social services. Retirement is a sublife for many of us.

> Life flashes before your eyes. Life is for the living.
> Live the Life of your dreams. One of Life's lessons
> is always moving on. It's okay to look back to see
> how far you've come but keep moving forward.

None of us have just one life if you look at it this way, and our life doesn't end when we lose our spouse or significant other. Of course, none of us would ever be convinced of that when it first happened, myself included. That's where the healing process of time comes in, time that provides us with wisdom and rationality.

> Don't take Life too seriously. Life is a series of
> natural and spontaneous changes. Our Life is
> what our thoughts make it. Life is funny. Things
> change, people change, but you will always be
> you.

Whatever numbered life we're on, we're living a life with purpose, kindness, appreciation, compassion, and understanding. We've become wiser, experienced, friendlier, and forgiving. We find ways to cope, believe, have faith, and hope. And we move forward knowing how richer all of our lives have become from spending the time we had with the one we loved.

> Everyone you meet is a part of your journey, but
> not all of them are meant to stay in your Life.
> Some people are just passing through to bring
> you gifts; either they're blessings or lessons.

Inside

If we never talk with anyone concerning our own personal feelings, thoughts, memories, or ambitions, no one will ever know what we are all about. Under regular circumstances such as everyday life, this can be a problem with our own socialization as an individual person, sibling, mother, father, friend. When you place grief in the situation, it takes on a whole new meaning that can have a significant effect on you and your behavior.

Keeping things inside is not healthy for you. Grief is very isolating, and the more times it is emphasized that you are not alone in your grief, the better we will be able to accept this and desire to share our thoughts and feelings with other like-minded people.

I look back at myself and consider that I am different, a man who was not in the least hesitant to tell people how much I was hurting, crying in public without fear, and asking for help from anyone who can guide me as to where to go and whom to call. I was searching to find some kind of comfort and relief to the pain I was experiencing.

Most men, not all, wouldn't be doing that. They would keep things inside. They would try to get through it on their own. They would ignore their feelings and inquiries from friends, coworkers, and family. They would lose sleep, have no appetite, refuse to seek medical advice or therapy, and be miserable and negative going forward. Some would act like it never happened despite the heartache they were experiencing and try to make immediate changes, proving to those around them that they are fine even though they really aren't. They don't want to be known that they can't handle this on their own even if it is destroying the person they are.

Most women, not all, wear their hearts on their sleeve and will be open and honest with how they are feeling after the loss of a loved one. I believe an incredible bond exists among women to help each other regardless of what the need is at the time. They will not keep it inside. They will share their fears and seek help and guidance from friends, family, and coworkers. They would seek medical attention if needed and certainly would feel more receptive to therapy or support. They realize that keeping things inside is harmful to them and their behavior and how they interact with others.

Those who know me, read my books, attended my support group, or hear me speak at events know that I am vocal about my own grief journey. I think it is important to share with others what we have been through. Through sharing, we can make a difference within ourselves and help others know that they are not alone and that there are so many of us out there who have been through similar situations that at one time seemed unbearable. By sharing, we can open the dialogue that everyone is afraid to talk about: death. It is such a part of life, and we need, as a society, to feel more comfortable talking about it.

I truly hope that we become better at this and stop keeping things inside. We need to be there for each other and remove the taboo of talking about death. Together, we can help each other heal.

Through the years

It's been more than a decade and a half since she died. That length of time is troublesome to me. I think of it as being far too long of time to be without her. And then I think with that much time since her death, was there an actual time I was with her? It's not like I am forgetting our life together, but time has a way of changing perspective in your mind and making you feel less at ease with your situation.

I knew her for thirty years, married for twenty-six and a half of those. Our marriage was a great partnership where our friendship preceded the time we fell in love and were united as one. It wasn't a perfect marriage. None are. We had our arguments and disagreements that led to no talking for a day or one of us in a room in solitude with the door closed. But we were always quick to respond to the foolishness of the reason for the disruption and resolved our conflict in a compassionate way. We were fortunate that conflicts did not happen that often, and most of our time together was happy and joyful.

I don't believe that anyone who has lost a loved one can say that their life has continued on uninterrupted from how it was since their death. It becomes different. Everything changes. Nothing stays the same. Even if you are fortunate enough to start another relationship or even remarry, your life is still different in many ways since the death of your beloved.

Grief will stay with you through the years. I'm not talking the gut-wrenching raw emotion that occurred in the first few days, weeks, or months of the loss you experienced. As time passes, the worst grief is softened and will eventually end up in the background of your life, possibly in your subconscious. It will come to the surface at times ever so gently as a reminder.

You will experience happiness again. You will smile and laugh again. And you will lead another life again, but not with them. You will always remember them and love them as you make choices for your future. Making choices always comes with risks, and there is that possibility of regrets at times. Don't let that discourage you. Everyday life is a risk, and without risk, there is no life to be had.

We all have stuff we like, collect, cherish, and through the years, you may be holding on to things that they loved and kept because you wanted to, and it seemed the right thing to do. Don't be surprised as years pass, the items you once thought you would never part with because they liked them, you will decide it is time to let go and part company. But until such a time crosses your path, hold on to them, and don't let anyone convince you otherwise.

Firsts will continue to happen way beyond the first year of your grief journey, and as long as you are open to them, you will recognize and acknowledge them. I notice all the things that I do or experience for the first time without her till this day. That is the one thing I wish I wasn't open to. I would become sad that it is yet one more thing I am experiencing alone and without them.

Triggers will continue to happen to you through the years. I look at triggers being either negative or positive. Positive triggers bring joy and allow you to smile when something comes to your attention. Negative triggers bring anxiety and make you feel stressed and sad. All triggers are sensory and emotional. The good news is that through the years, you will eventually have more positive joy triggers than negative anxiety triggers.

Ultimately, it is entirely up to you to feel better about the life ahead of you. Yes, you are in control even though you think you are not. In the beginning of this grief journey, we are all out of control without any compass. Eventually, it comes down to your will and believing. Your will to heal and love is the strongest emotion that any of us have at our disposal. Along with faith and hope, you are responsible for your well-being, and you will succeed in this life you are now dealt with.

Down the Rabbit Hole

Let's think about life and the time we have to be part of it all. How often do we think in any situation that the outcome of something was dependent on making a right instead of a left. Deciding to leave five minutes later instead of on time. Taking a short cut to a destination instead of the long way. How different would things have turned out, or would they?

In many cases, the course of your life is held in the balance, and it could really come down to one decision, one risk, one choice, one fleeting moment of time when you picked or chose or decided the way you would approach a situation that would then take you to all the other things that will now come from that initial choice on your part. And that also works the opposite way as well. Not deciding that would make the outcome very different as would choosing something totally different than the first choice you made.

After you made that decision and things turn out fairly well in your opinion, you become grateful. I guess if it didn't, you'd ponder, *What if your decision was the opposite?* Or you could also think, *What if I chose to do nothing and keep things the way they were?*

Whatever the case may be, most of us go with a gut feeling. We feel that after considering all the options that are available at the time (I hope we do this), we decide on the best thing for us that feels right. We are confident in ourselves and our decision, and we move forward with the choice we made and don't look back. That is really the only way to do this.

Afterword

I have grown older and wiser when it comes to grief, but I still don't have all the answers, and no one ever will. We all must live our life in the best way possible that works for us. How you spend time will shape the contours of your life. If you pay attention and learn, you will find who you are and your essential reason for being here. This is something that took years for me to figure out. I am hoping that for anyone else, it will take less time and you will be able to feel better sooner than I did.

Without the changes that have taken place throughout my journey, there is no telling the kind of condition I would be in physically, mentally, emotionally, and spiritually. Listen to your instinct, your gut and nothing else. Be open to your own thoughts and feelings while allowing them inside your inner circle of being. Meditate about it. Pray. You will know when it is time to do the next thing. Then don't fear doing it. Take the risk. Choose with confidence. Make the change happen.

Changes 1 and 2 happened because I listened to what my instinct was telling me about what the next step was, and within those changes there was more happening to guide me to other places. Change 3 was inevitable but not desired. The loss of my dog Hal put me in one of the darkest places I have ever been but not before his unconditional love, devotion, and companionship made the first decade or so without my wife tolerable. This final change forced me out of a comfort zone I was grateful for since Hal was her dog. Hal's presence allowed me to get through the first two changes and enjoy the memory of my wife through him. It was time for me to be on my own now and be capable of leading this new life of mine, forever keeping my wife Sue and our dog Hal in loving memory.

Live life to the fullest. Do not take your loved ones for granted. Be kind. Be grateful. Be positive. Journal your thoughts and feelings. Help others when you can. Please know that you are not alone in whatever hardship you are facing at the moment. Don't fear asking for guidance and help. Keep love in your heart and joy in your soul. Each and every day is a gift.

Acknowledgments

For their patience, knowledge, compassion, and experience helping me in my weakest moments and being able to encourage me to overcome my fear, anxiety, and uncertainty:

Therapists and bereavement professionals

For their acceptance of me in a nonjudgmental environment that was simple, free to attend, and allowed me to express my thoughts, cry, or stay silent as I tried to cope with the hurt and sorrow of my incomprehensible loss:

Grief support groups

For their faith and interest in coming to explore and participate in a grief support group created by a nontherapist to help people heal from the loss of a spouse or significant other:

Attendees present and past of the sudSSpirit grief support group

About the Author

Dominic Murgido earned multiple degrees in criminal justice, instructed college courses as an adjunct professor, and is a master coffee roaster. He retired from careers in retail loss prevention and social services. He founded sudSSpirit, a bereavement support group, a few years after the sudden, unexpected death of his wife. He publishes a quarterly newsletter of the same name.

Besides being a grief advocate who provides support and solace to those who are grieving, Dominic is also an advocate for safe driving by providing awareness and a voice to legislators to increase education and training for safe-driving practices as well as penalties as they relate to traffic violations that cause injury and death.

Dominic is also a writer, editor, commentator, and highly regarded speaker. His other books include *In a Heartbeat: A Tale of Reflection, Faith, Hope, and Resilience* (a memoir) and *Miss Your Forever: Reflections after the Death of a Spouse*. He can be reached at dominicmurgido.com.